Praise for Teaching College

"A really useful book for any college professor who wants to move beyond lectures and give students deeper engagement. A practical, easy to read, and important guide for anyone in higher education."

- **JO BOALER**, Professor of Mathematics Education, Stanford University, best-selling author of *Mathematical Mindsets*, and co-founder of YouCubed.org

"This is a terrific collection of tried and true teaching strategies that, unlike most other books on university teaching, is written for the adjunct or contingent university teacher, by someone who's been there. Norman Eng understand the constraints that contingent faculty teach under, and has created a book to help them succeed."

- **KAREN KELSKY**, best-selling author, founder, and president of *The Professor Is In*

"Dr. Eng has created an accessible, evidence based guide to effective college instruction that will be particularly valuable for relatively new faculty members who are coming out of graduate programs where there were limited opportunities to teach. He provides practical guidance and anticipates and responds to the numerous challenges all instructors face. This is a very valuable resource, and I encourage its widespread use."

- **DAVID H. MONK**, Dean, College of Education, Penn State University

"A great resource for college instructors who are interested in excellent teaching—accessible, practical, and full of actionable research-based suggestions."

- **YONG ZHAO**, Foundation Distinguished Professor, School of Education, University of Kansas

"This book is an excellent source for instructors who would like to take their first steps toward including interactive and hands-on work in their classes, which when done effectively can powerfully shape student learning. In addition, the important support that the book offers for successfully implementing these beginning interactive approaches can give innovative instructors the confidence and inspiration they need to take further steps toward mastering ever more challenging and rewarding approaches to effective teaching."

- **GRETCHEN JOHNSON**, Dean, School of Education, City College of New York, City University of New York

"*Teaching College* is chock-full of essential information to help you to make a paradigm shift in how you present your material, from understanding the common problems when lecturing and "touching" your audience to use slides as support - everything that you do can either create or destroy a learning experience."

- **READERS' FAVORITE** review

"Norman Eng writes as if he has been teaching his whole life. This fresh voice talks to both students and teachers imploring them to develop introspection and curiosity. Eng challenges his readers to cultivate their own abilities. In a conversational tone that is rare and profound in an age that honors reductive and simplistic solutions, the author does not write a "how to" book but one that calls for teachers and students to think deeply as they engage with educational issues."

- **KAREL ROSE**, Professor, Brooklyn College, School of Education, CUNY Graduate Center

"College instructors are rarely provided with explicit instruction in how to teach effectively. As a university faculty member for more than two decades, I remain puzzled by this phenomenon. Like author Norman Eng, I learned most of what I know about teaching from my experience in a teacher preparation program, as an elementary teacher, and through trial-and-error in college classrooms. Most university instructors, however, have not had the first two experiences and a number of them, in my experience, do not change how they teach to a great degree over the course of their careers. In this highly readable and well-organized text, Dr. Eng shares stories and specific examples from his own teaching and provides practical suggestions and action steps for college instructors seeking to enhance their effectiveness in working with students. As a lifelong teacher, I learned many strategies—including how to write a more effective syllabus, alternatives to lectures, and ways to actively engage students in learning—that I am eager to try after reading *Teaching College*. This book will appeal to both novice instructors and seasoned professors and would be especially useful for faculty members to read and discuss in groups in order to continue their professional growth and development as teachers, conversations we pursue far too infrequently in higher education."

- **APRIL BEDFORD**, Dean, School of Education, Brooklyn College, City University of New York

"The practical strategies in the book is what's missing in higher ed. No other book helps college instructors with such step-by-step detail. A must read for the novice (and even seasoned) college instructor."

"*Teaching College* is the most 'bang for your buck' resource that I have seen for new college instructors. His advice is evidence-based and very practical. You can't go wrong with this book. Highly recommended."

"What a fantastic book! As someone who has taught in K-12 and college classrooms, I have often lamented the fact that K-12 teachers get so much preparation in the skills of teaching, while those at the college level get none. In *Teaching College*, Norman Eng closes that gap brilliantly, synthesizing education and marketing into a fresh approach that will significantly change the way college classes are taught worldwide. You will find useful insights and practical, actionable tips on every page, and all of it written in an approachable, conversational style. A must for anyone who teaches at the college level."

TEACHING COLLEGE

DOWNLOAD THE
AUDIOBOOK FREE!

Just to say thanks for buying my book, I would like to give you the audiobook version FREE!

TO DOWNLOAD, GO TO:

http://normaneng.org/tc/audiobook

TEACHING COLLEGE

The Ultimate Guide to Lecturing, Presenting,
and Engaging Students

Norman Eng, Ed.D.

Teaching College
The Ultimate Guide to Lecturing,
Presenting, and Engaging Students

Copyright © 2017 Norman Eng
ALL RIGHTS RESERVED

ISBN-13: 978-0-9985875-1-6 | ISBN-10: 0-9985875-1-6
Cover Design: Archangel Ink

To my family and friends:
You know who you are.
Thank you for your support.

To my K–12 and university colleagues:
Thank you for your wisdom.

TABLE OF CONTENTS

INTRODUCTION

Have you ever found yourself thinking:

I'm frustrated that students aren't doing the reading.

Getting my students to participate is like pulling teeth!

I'm on my own here. Who can I turn to for teaching support?

My students like me, but I'm not sure if they're really learning.

I have to teach a course. Now what?

I need a good course evaluation.

I thought I was a good teacher …

Why am I still doing most of the talking in class?

I know teaching is important, but I don't have time to plan.

My students are more focused on texting and surfing online than paying attention.

I want to be the best, but I don't know where to begin.

My teaching is fine—it's the students who don't care.

Help! My students are bored.

Aren't college students supposed to be mature enough to take learning seriously?

My students seem to be learning, but something is still missing.

Sometimes I feel like they just do the bare requirements. I want them to want more!

Students just want the A—they don't care about mastering the material.

If any of these thoughts have crossed your mind, you're not alone. Teaching in higher education is hard when you care. Unfortunately, there are two big problems: 1) *Your students don't care about your course*; and 2) *most college instructors (including full-time professors!) don't know how to teach.*

To address the first problem: students are busy. Possibly overwhelmed. But they do still care about doing well. Nonetheless, with up to four other courses, a low-paying job, a budding social life, the stresses of building a career, and family responsibilities—not to mention the distractions of social media—undergraduates have competing priorities.[1] Unless your course connects with students in some way, they won't invest beyond the requirements.

Second: college instructors don't ever learn how to teach. There is no training program or teaching license requirements as there are for their K–12 (kindergarten through Grade 12) counterparts. Graduate and doctoral programs focus exclusively on cultivating subject matter expertise. While that helps professors do research, it doesn't qualify them to mold impressionable minds.

So we learn to teach by imitating what our professors did—we lecture. In fact, lecturing is still the most dominant form of instruction in college,[*] with over half of faculty using it in all or most of their classes.[2] Evidence, however, shows that traditional stand-and-deliver lectures do little to help students learn,[3] much less retain what they have learned.

Making the problem worse is the fact that more and more college faculty are contingent (part time or non-tenure track professors). At least 50 percent are adjunct instructors.[4] Aside from job instability, contingent faculty lack the administrative support that full-time, tenured faculty receive, such as securing copies of required textbooks and student email addresses, limited access to professional development courses, and the ability to participate in departmental meetings.[5] This makes it hard to ensure consistent, quality instruction.

What happens when you combine a lack of pedagogical training with student indifference? A crisis in higher education. In their book *Academically Adrift: Limited Learning on College Campuses*, sociologists Richard Arum and Josipa Roksa found that almost half of U.S. students don't improve their reasoning or writing skills during the first two years of college. And after four years, more than one-third of students (36%) still show no real gains. Furthermore,

---

[*] While lectures are still the main form of instruction (see Goffe and Kauper, 2014; Macdonald, Manduca, Mogk, and Tewksbury, 2005; Smith and Valentine, 2012), the use of discussions has expanded significantly over the past two decades (Eagan et al., 2014)

traditional lectures simply do not foster real-world skills like innovating, collaborating, and continuous learning.[6] What then is the point of attending college? No wonder today's graduates are unprepared for the real world, according to employers.[7]

As a college instructor, you can change this.

The Solution: Learn from Marketers and K–12 Teachers

While you can't control institutional factors at the university level (i.e., funding, culture, etc.), you can get students to care more. You can also learn to teach effectively. This book shows you how, by adopting the approaches used in two industries—*marketing* and *K–12 education.*

Marketers *know* how to reach audiences. They are experts when it comes to building relationships and making consumers care. How? By figuring out what they need, what frustrates them—and then solving that problem. Google, for instance, streamlined information search. Amazon simplified online buying. Uber and Airbnb did the same for car service and accommodations, respectively. Netflix solved on-demand streaming media. The entrepreneurs behind these behemoths were salespeople who knew how to market their products and services.

As an educator, you are doing the same. In his book, *To Sell Is Human: The Surprising Truth About Moving Others*, psychologist Daniel H. Pink argues that teachers are sellers of ideas. That's how you inspire students and change their behavior. Therefore, without the ability to finger your students' problems, you won't solve them.

Do you actually know what keeps your students up at night? What problems they face in life, in school, and in your class? This book shows you the secrets marketers use to uncover their audience's problems, build relationships, and connect with their customers.

The other industry professors can learn from is K–12 education. The best schoolteachers know which pedagogical tools and strategies engage students. For instance, they use *exit tickets* as one way to check if students are actually learning. They use *cold-calling* to improve student participation. They cultivate a safe and supportive classroom community as the first order of business. These are just a few of the many K–12 principles you will learn to enhance your pedagogical effectiveness by a factor of ten.

Also, simply knowing how to teach is not enough. You'd be surprised how many education professors—who supposedly know the latest pedagogical approaches—can't seem to connect with their students. The reverse is also true. Knowing how to communicate doesn't mean knowing how to teach. You can't be effective without knowing the right instructional methods to use.[*]

As a former marketing executive and K–12 teacher, I've applied the perspectives from both industries to college teaching with astounding results. *Teaching College: The Ultimate Guide to Lecturing,*

---

[*] While both the ability to teach and the ability to communicate are necessary, I believe the latter is even more critical. If professors thought more like marketers, they would be more effective teachers.

Presenting, and Engaging Students captures these insights into a concise guide for the busy and frustrated instructor who wants to supercharge their pedagogy *now*.

If you follow this guide, you will improve. Students will raise their hands more, invest in their assignments, and give you better end-of-term evaluations. Even better, you can read this book today and implement the strategies tomorrow—even if you've already defined your syllabus for the semester. With this clear step-by-step guide, you will have an advantage over other instructors in your department—including established professors. All you have to do is keep reading and following the action steps. Each chapter will give you new insight as you strive to become the best instructor. Don't wait. Your students—and your reputation—depend on it.

Is This Book for You?

If you are an early career instructor or professor, then this book is for you. This may include graduate (or teaching) assistants, assistant professors, adjunct instructors, or other contingent faculty who have less pedagogical experience and want a practical, step-by-step guide to conducting a college class. *Teaching College* is meant to help you, the busy instructor see teaching as communicating and connecting—two areas top marketers and K–12 teachers do consistently.

However, seasoned instructors—including tenured professors—can also benefit from the contents in this book. Most will not have undergone pedagogical training and can leverage this book's marketing and K–12 approaches/strategies.

Teaching College is not for those who consider teaching less important than their scholarly (research) endeavors. It is also not for those who believe good teaching is instinctive—that some professors simply have "it" while others don't. Every single effective teacher I've come across regularly reflects on and refines his or her craft.

Keep in Mind as You Read …

Like teaching, this book is not "one-size-fits-all." No instructional guide can be. Some strategies work best for small classes whereas others can work for large, lecture-hall classes. You as the instructor have to find which ones work best with your particular situation and your individual disposition. Similarly, some courses, such as those in social science and STEM(science, technology, engineering, and math), may lend themselves more easily to strategies in this book but professors in liberal arts courses have also validated many of these strategies. The marketer's mindset discussed in Chapter 2, for instance, applies across the board, whether the class has 350 students or is focused on music theory. That one approach can dramatically improve the way you teach, no matter the size of the class or the discipline.

Although these ideas have been tested and validated through experience and research, this book is not, nor is it intended to be, viewed the same as peer-reviewed research. I simply want to pass along what two industries—business marketing and K–12 education—have taught me.

As such, I write without academic jargon. Footnotes are used, citations are given, and claims are made without phrases like "these data suggest…"

"Pro Tips" are provided throughout the book. These tactics and ideas are based on years of trial-and-error and can save you time and frustration. Each pro tip is highlighted with a graphic of a graduation cap/light bulb.

At the end of the book, I recommend specific books, links, or resources (and highlight those that are free). I do *not* get paid to do this. In other words, I do not use affiliate marketing to direct traffic to another site and earn commission for referrals. You can be assured that my recommendations are based solely on quality and content.

I will update this book to reflect my continued experiences as well as the latest research in neuroscience, pedagogy/education, child/human development, and communication. More than anything else, I want to spread the message about the importance of teaching, particularly at the collegiate level. Universities across the US are the envy of the world, but truthfully, that is due more to the reputation borne from the research coming out of the universities than the teaching. If we can apply that same rigor to our instruction, then more students will learn and thrive in the twenty-first century global society. I want as many teachers as possible—instructors, lecturers, adjuncts, and assistant professors—to read this book and apply its message to their classroom.

This book does not and cannot cover everything. Certain "progressive" approaches to teaching, such as *team-based learning* (TBL), *project-based learning* (PBL), the *flipped classroom*, and *online instruction* are not covered. While I see them powerfully shaping student learning in the future, they require extensive professional development training or, at the very least, a dedicated book. Unfortunately, the existing nature of higher education academia, with its emphasis on publishing and other professional responsibilities, makes it hard for professors to invest in teaching as K–12 teachers do. Furthermore, adjuncts and instructors have less access to departmental support than their tenured counterparts. This makes it harder to streamline good pedagogy.

This guide, therefore, aims to *meet busy instructors where they are.* This means improving lectures by incorporating more interactive and hands-on work. Helping instructors redo their syllabi. Implementing strategies to encourage student participation.

As a final note, this book is a work in progress. Not everything here will work for every instructor or student. In fact, making peace with the idea that sometimes a student will not receive your approach or strategy well has helped me see how much more there is to learn. Implementing the best strategies does *not* guarantee every student will suddenly learn more effectively in a given semester or that instructors will receive significantly higher departmental or student evaluations. In fact, research suggests that "active learning," the kind of approach this book argues for, works only when instructors know how to use it.[8] Simply incorporating debates or games may engage students more, but their excitement can also mask actual learning. The point is to use the recommendations in this book as a starting point and build from experience. In the end, I guarantee you will be significantly more effective than you were yesterday.

The insights and strategies you're about to read have been proven to create positive, long-lasting results. As you read, consider how they might be applied to your particular course(s). OK, enough of this. Let's get to it.

PART 1

Lay the Groundwork

CHAPTER 1

Understand the Common Problems of Lecturing

"For class today I'll be reading the PowerPoint
word for word for word."
—Every professor, everywhere.
(@CollegeGirlHumor, June 16, 2013)

Irreverent it may be, but this tweet captures how frustrated college students feel about their professors.[*] Many feel their professors aren't teaching at all, in the sense they are not helping students understand, internalize, and apply what they read. Instead, they feel instructors regurgitate too much information from the texts. Too often,

---

[*] Note I use the terms *professor*, *instructor*, *adjunct*, and *lecturer* interchangeably, even though there are clear distinctions. I will typically use *instructor* as a catchall for anyone teaching a college course, including graduate assistants. In the end, students see us as *professors*. I will specify among the terms where necessary.

instructors rely on PowerPoint or one-sided lectures that leave students bored and disengaged.

The result? Little to no learning.

In talks on pedagogy, teaching expert Eric Mazur asks audiences to think about something they are really good at, like a skill. He then asks them to think about *how* they became really good at that skill, whether by trial and error, apprenticeship, lectures, or advice from family and friends. The largest group, about 60 percent, selected "practicing" as the route to mastery.

Zero percent chose lectures.[9] "The danger with lucid lectures ... is that they create the illusion of teaching for teachers, and the illusion of learning for learners," Mazur summarized.[10] Lectures, at least in the traditional sense, rarely help.

So what exactly constitutes a lecture? Most instructors see it in terms of the teacher talking most of the time, interspersed with the occasional question or short discussion. Purists, however, see lectures as "continuous expositions by the speaker who wants the audience to learn something."[11] For this book, I am referring to both above definitions when talking about lectures—expositions by the teacher that *dominate* class sessions (think big lecture halls) as well as those that *largely make up* the class.

So, what are some of the common problems that plague bad lectures? Based on informal discussions with students and colleagues, as well as research and experience, I explore three main issues below. Which one characterizes your lectures?

Problem #1: Lectures That Are Too Dense or Too Long

In my first year teaching a foundations course, I used the PowerPoint template that came with the instructor's copy of the textbook. I didn't know any better. It gave me a much-needed lesson structure. The problem was the slides took 45 minutes to cover, if not longer. Students were nodding off, checking their phones and yawning. They would frequently "go to the bathroom." Even though the class clearly liked me, they wanted more "hands-on" work (read: *practice* and *experience*), according to evaluations. That hit me hard, because I take criticisms personally.

Dense and long lectures tend to duplicate the material from assigned readings. *Today, I'll be going over the major concepts from this week's reading* ... Sound familiar? The instructor hopes to explain and clarify the material so that students can recall it for papers and tests. Often, such lectures take up most if not all of the class. Here are three signs your lecture is too dense and/or too long: 1) When taking notes is the primary thing students do in class; 2) when students appear bored or sleepy; and/or 3) when they cannot summarize what they just learned at the end of class or the following class. (Have you ever checked? We'll talk about *exit slips* in Chapter 10.)

So why do we lecture so much? Usually, it's to cover the textbook or the curriculum. We want students to know, or at least be familiar with, all the core concepts and figures associated with a given topic.[*] My phys-ed majors complain about having to memorize all the parts of the human body for their required physiology class. It's tedious when the instructor just explicates the function of every muscle and bone, they say.

But it's only ninety minutes, you may be thinking. No. Students hear lecture after lecture after lecture—every day. No wonder they retain so little of what you say, no matter how clearly you say it. Studies find students retain less than 30 percent of what they hear.[12] In many cases, they barely know more by the end of the semester than students who've never even take the course—only 8 percent more, in one study of psychology students.[13]

Furthermore, students have lives that don't revolve around instructors' perfectly planned lectures (sorry, but it's true). Novice instructors who love their discipline often make the mistake of planning for the "ideal" student[14]—one who reads their overly long syllabi (most don't), does complex assignments correctly the first time (which rarely happens), or answers questions thoughtfully and critically. Real students are working, caring for siblings, and taking five other courses—all of which also require their undivided attention. You can't expect them to be mentally present all the time.

---

[*] Weimer (2002) describes this common teaching perspective as the "more is better" approach (p. 46)

Think about the oral presentations you assign in class. I've observed classrooms where a student presents a topic—say, for instance, the theory of multiple intelligences—where she *shoehorns* every detail about the theorist behind it, including when he was born and what influenced his work.

While appropriate for a biography essay, it is completely inappropriate as a presentation, because it serves no benefit to the rest of the class. The presenter, after all, only cares about demonstrating how much she knows to the evaluator—you. She has no interest in engaging her classmates. Her text-heavy slides reflect this mindset. Have you ever looked around the room during student presentations? It's agonizing. The rest of the class couldn't care less. They'd rather you teach.

One rule of thumb schoolteachers use to determine appropriate lesson length is to take the children's age and double it. So, if you're teaching seven-year olds (around second grade), you shouldn't spend more than fifteen minutes talking before they lose focus. Often times, it is even less, which is why many teachers even use the *age rule* to plan lessons: seven-year-olds shouldn't have to sit still for more than seven minutes at a time on a task.

These rules are unproven, but they are meant to give you an idea. Developmentally, children simply can't sit still for long, nor can they remember much after that. Adults aren't that different. Long periods of talking will make them squirm. Studies confirm this. College students' attention starts high at the beginning and peaks around fifteen to twenty minutes into a lecture.[15] They retain 70 percent of the information in the first ten minutes of a lecture but only 20 percent in the last ten minutes.[16] After that, they go into a "brain drift." Attention never returns.

As such, didactic lectures should remain bite-sized and interspersed. Even if you add in "new" material not covered in the text, it should be concise and relevant. Add in other *modalities*, such as discussions, questions, and activities throughout—something we will go over in Chapter 6, *Engage Your Audience.*

In short: College students love a change of pace just as much as kids. Get them out of their seats.

Problem #2: Lectures Disconnected from Students

Related to long and dense lectures are those that are one-sided affairs. When professors employ the traditional "direct instruction" approach, students can't relate to the topic or concepts being taught. They become passive learners. A famous quote attributed to Benjamin Franklin (but in fact taken from Chinese Confucian philosopher Xunzi) says, "Tell me and I forget. Teach me and I remember. Involve me and I learn." Students gain by being active, rather than passive, learners.

Lectures need to relate to students' lives, which explains why we have to know our intended audience. Making a topic relevant will make it interesting, like connecting the Civil War with sibling fights.

On the flip side, just because a fact is interesting doesn't make it relevant. For example, it might be nice to know that the small intestines are 23 feet long (7 meters) … but who cares? Unless it relates to the audience's needs, then it remains just that—an interesting fact.

Part of the problem is what psychologists call the "curse of knowledge,"[17] or the "expert blind spot."[18] This is an egocentric tendency (particularly among intellectuals) to overestimate what our audience knows. As disciplinary scholars, we take for granted standard industry terms like *regression*, *implications*, and *literature review*, because we tend to forget how hard it was to learn something once we know it. Think of it like giving directions. I think I'm being clear when I tell a tourist on the New York City subway to "go to the other side of the platform and take the downtown R train to SoHo." Yet the other person's probably thinking, *First of all, what do you mean by "the other side"? Does the R train only go downtown or are all downtown trains R trains? What stop is SoHo?* Tourists operate from limited background knowledge.

Yet we often forget that. Students come in with all levels of knowledge and literacies about our discipline, and our high-level jargon flies over their heads. And they won't admit being confused. Students just jot notes and hope to make sense of them later. If you ever hear your students saying, "I think I understand this," that means they *don't* (physicist Richard Feynman once said something similar). We can't assume students get what we say. Connecting with them *where they are*—not where they ought to be—is more important.[19]

Problem #3: Lectures That Rely On Slides

Finally, too many instructors hide behind slideware like PowerPoint. One study found that a majority of sociology professors (55%) reported using PowerPoint frequently (meaning at least 75 percent of class meetings) or always.[20] Of those students, 66 percent say their professors use PowerPoint in all or most of their class sessions.

Although useful, slides aren't supposed to replace the lecture. Students seem to agree, if the following comments (posted via Twitter and elsewhere) are any indication:

Being a college professor would be easy. Read off a PowerPoint you made 10 years ago and give online quizzes with questions you googled [sic]. (@Blazik, March 27, 2013)

I hate when a professor makes class mandatory and reads straight from the PowerPoint instead of actually teaching … I can do that at home. (@Breannedwards)

Y'all ever sat in a class, copied every word down off the power point [sic], and still not kno [sic] a damn thing the professor said? (@_BlkSuperMan, Febraury 7, 2014)

I frequently write down blindly anything that is written on the PowerPoint without absorbing it until studying for the test. Also, when I'm copying down the PowerPoint words I'm not usually listening to the instructor. Power Point minimizes the engagement I have with a class and instead condenses it into a few slides with bullet points.[21]

On the other hand, professors do have their reasons for using PowerPoint. It organizes our thoughts, structures our lessons, and helps us remember what to say. Textbook publishers like Pearson know this, so they include ready-made lecture slides with their teacher editions of textbooks. It's tempting for professors to use them and maybe even tweak them (I know I have). On the whole, however, ready-made slides harm teaching and learning, as one computer science student blogger asserts:

> The problem is that when the professor does not [create his or her own] presentation, they run the risk of sounding like they don't know what they're talking about. My current Operating Systems professor suffers from this. As each new slide comes up, he takes a second to read it and then starts with, "Okay, what this slide is talking about is ..." or "What they mean by this is ..." As opposed to explaining the material himself, it sounds like he just expects us to read the slides, and then let him elaborate.[22]

No wonder PowerPoint is considered the most significant teaching factor contributing to boredom![23] Avoid using (or even adapting) ready-made slides. However, if you know how to incorporate PowerPoint into your lecture, it can powerfully facilitate student engagement and learning. This will be covered in Chapter 8, *Use Slides as Support.*

Despite all the problems with lectures, of which the above are only the most common, I am not against them. Lectures can move audiences when done properly. The TEDTalks events, where people present "ideas worth sharing," is one example where lectures clearly work. As one professor stated,

> I have never believed that there was intrinsic damage being done to students in what has been called the "sage on the stage" model of teaching. I don't think it's always bad to listen to an expert talk about what she knows best, and I don't think that the discussion format is inherently better than the lecture format merely because the latter allows the students to express their opinions. On the contrary, I think that a truly great lecturer has the capacity to change a student's life, and I think that there is something valuable in students listening to a person who has an effortless command of a subject, in seeing the kind of dedication and erudition a fine lecturer embodies.[24]

The key, then, is to maximize your lecture. We'll get to that in Chapter 5, *Develop Your Topic*.

Summary and Action Step

To wrap up, lectures that are too dense/long, disconnected, or overly rely on slides can undermine student learning and engagement. Other problems exist, such as poor classroom management, but can be remedied with the right approach— something we discuss in the next chapter—and a well-structured, prepared lesson.

So, here are two action steps to take:

1. Ask yourself what mistakes you have made or have seen too many times in lectures and presentations that hurt student engagement. List 3–5 of them. It will help you recognize your shortcomings and steer clear of them when we move into the next segment.

2. Find a topic you teach and have that ready for the next chapter. For example, I teach a course on child development, so one topic I would teach is Jean Piaget's theory of cognitive development.

The next chapter, *Focus on the Student, Not the Content*, will change how you approach your course—I guarantee it.

CHAPTER 2

Focus on the Student, Not the Content

In the last chapter, we saw some of the common problems that plague bad lectures and presentations, such as when instructors engage in direct instruction the whole period, cram too much material, fail to connect with students, and rely too much on slides. When this happens, students lose interest and you lose their respect.

So what's the better approach?

It starts by understanding the *psychology* behind good teaching. This is the most important part of the book. If you don't understand how top professors think, it won't matter how good your PowerPoint or activities are.

When I left advertising, I took away three life-changing lessons:

1. Know your target audience.
2. Consider the big picture first.
3. Determine the main benefit to the audience.

Let's explore each lesson and find practical ways to apply them to your course.

Know Your Target Audience

If you don't know what your customers need, they will never pay attention to your ads, your product, or your service, no matter how good it is. Teaching works the same way. You are marketing your knowledge to students no differently than executives at Wieden+Kennedy are marketing to Nike customers. Daniel H. Pink, in his book *To Sell Is Human: The Surprising Truth About Moving Others*, argues that this ability to market your work is increasingly important in a social economy—where Facebook, Instagram, and Sina Weibo reign. Teaching, Pink points out, revolves around "non-sales" selling, which depend more on the "creative, heuristic, problem-finding skills of artists than on the reductive, algorithmic, problem-finding skills of technicians."[25] It is more than simply *conveying knowledge.*

Instead, teaching starts by knowing your students, as this group of undergraduates wrote to their professors:

> … instead of imagining what students are thinking, get to know us. Find out what college is like for us *now*, rather than what it was like for you years ago. Learn that we respond to your lecture very individually, and that we pick our lectures often for the individuality of the professor rather than the subject. Condemning or celebrating the lecture isn't, in the end, as useful as understanding what we need. So please ask us. Because

we've had enough of sitting silently in the dark, listening to all of you talk.[26]

(This excerpt came from an essay written by fifteen undergraduates to their professors, titled "A Lecture From the Lectured.")

Research supports a *student-centered approach*. Why? Because students filter your lectures through their own experiences and knowledge. They are like the fish in Leo Lionni's children's story *Fish is Fish*, who, upon being told of the world beyond the pond, imagines people as fish who walk on their tailfins, birds as fish with wings, and cows as fish with udders.[27] No matter how the world was described to him, the fish only sees the world through his perspective.

The point is, people connect new knowledge with what they already know.[28] So when professors start lecturing above the students' heads, learners have no experiences to connect to. Instead, start from where students are. Activate their prior knowledge to see what they know, so that you can fill in the gaps. This will ensure students learn more readily.

Yet too many instructors "cover the material" rather than *teach* it. Just because you feel drained at the end of a vigorous lecture doesn't mean you've been an active teacher—just that you've made lecturing more about you and the content rather than about the students. You need to uncover the wants, needs, and level of the students—*your* target audience. If too many students are daydreaming or texting, chances are your lectures are simply not connecting with them.

To figure out their mindset, ask yourself these seven questions posed by presentation expert Nancy Duarte (2008):

1. What is your audience like?
2. Why are they here?
3. What keeps them up at night?
4. How can you solve their problem?
5. What do you want them to do?
6. How might they resist?
7. How can you best reach them?

Although these questions were meant for business presentations—selling a product or service—they are instructive. They create a profile of your student group, of which you as an instructor need to be aware. Marketers call this the *ideal client profile* (ICP), which captures the demographic data (age, gender, college major/minor, socioeconomic/financial aid status, family size, employment, etc.) and psychographic data (values, beliefs, fears, behavioral style) of their audience in one paragraph. Any effective ad has to target its ICP. Here's one profile I created for my child development course:

My ideal client profile (ICP) is a twenty-year-old Latina from a working-class family who commutes to college, lives with her parents, and works part time. She works hard but is often overwhelmed because she takes five classes per semester in order to qualify for financial aid. She has one younger sibling and is concerned with passing the new, harder teacher certification and the teacher performance assessments. Although she loves working with children, she is not sure if she can handle the rigors of teaching in an urban public school classroom, with its diverse student needs.

Notice how laser-focused this profile is. It is describing one person, not a group, which is similar to how author Stephen King approaches his writing. All his books are written with one "Ideal Reader" in mind—his wife Tabitha. Why? An ideal reader reminds us that we're writing for *that person*, not for the author. It keeps us focused, grounded, and accountable to that person. "Try to imagine whether he or she will be bored ... if you know the tastes of your [Ideal Reader] even half as well as I know the tastes of mine, that shouldn't be too hard," wrote King in his acclaimed book, *On Writing: A Memoir of the Craft.*

Knowing my ideal client profile allowed me to emphasize the following in my course:

- Writing prompts that prepare students to pass the newer, more rigorous state certification tests.

- Opportunities to *practice* teaching regularly, rather than merely *learn* how to teach.

- Discussions of students' fieldwork observations in public school classrooms, including how to address behavior issues and lack of participation.

- Apply the topics of child development, such as Erikson's

Eight Stages of Life, to the classroom context, rather than merely lecturing about it.

While these are broad considerations, knowing your target audience can even help you in the day-to-day interactions with students. In my theory-based Foundations of Education course one semester, many students had trouble understanding *cultural literacy*, a term coined by educator E.D. Hirsch, Jr. Technically, it refers to the ability to understand and participate fully in a given culture; but really, what does this actually *mean*? More importantly, why is *cultural literacy* even important? I wasn't sure how to convey this.

That's when I remembered who my target audience was: about 40 percent were student-athletes that semester, which gave me an idea for the next class.

"Stan," I called to one of the student-athletes (not his real name), "you've been following the New York Knicks recently?" We were about to do a little role-playing.

"Yeah."

"What's the team's overall field goal percentage?"

"I dunno, but it's not that good. Less than .400 for sure."

"How'd Carmelo do last night?"

"I think he was like eight of seventeen or something."

We went back and forth the next few minutes as sports fans

do—talking about who had the best "jumper," who could do a good "pick-and-roll," and who grabbed the most "offensive rebounds." As the marquee player on the university's basketball team, Stan had no problem talking shop.

The rest of the class watched quizzically, perhaps wondering what this had to do with *cultural literacy*. Precisely what I wanted.

Turning to the class, I asked, "Is there anyone here who *doesn't* follow sports?"

A quarter of the class raised their hands.

I zeroed in on one young woman. "Jen, did you understand any of this?"

"Uh … not really," she replied tentatively.

"But how can that be? We *were* speaking English, no?"

The light bulbs began to go off. The non-sports fans in the class had just experienced what it felt like to be "culturally illiterate"—not being able to understand or participate fluently in a given culture (in this case, basketball) even though they spoke the language. The feeling of being left out rang powerfully as a lesson: When you aren't familiar with the cultural content, you can't engage fully.

"It's kind of like sitting at the kids table," summarized one student. Everyone laughed.

This turned into a whole discussion about how hard it is to get a job, vote, and build social and professional relationships without *cultural literacy*. If students had merely read about it, they would not have internalized this concept as deeply. Lecturing certainly didn't do much—I tried and failed. They needed to experience the concept first hand. Leveraging my students' interests or disinterests in sports helped me connect with them through role-play.

So, what is the ideal client profile (ICP) for your course? In other words, what kind of student takes your course? Use the following questions to generate your answers:

- How old is this (typical) student?
- Does he work? (What kind of job?)
- What is her background—ethnically, culturally, and socioeconomically?
- What is his biggest fear, concern, or obstacle in regard to this course/program?
- What is this student's best way of learning? What does she expect? What does he need?

One last thing to consider is the kind of learners in your classroom. Teaching scholar Ken Bain summarized three types:[29]

1. *Surface learners*: the ones who just want to get out of the course alive. They choose the easiest courses and are loathe to put much critical thought into their work. They prefer to

memorize information and repeat it on the examination.

2. *Strategic learners*: students who tend to be concerned with status and recognition, such as high GPA. As a result, they put in the work, but tend to take less risk for fear of jeopardizing their status. They want the right procedures to follow, but do not necessarily understand the concept behind the work.

3. *Deep learners*: In contrast, these students grapple with ideas, concepts, and implications and welcome opportunities to think critically. They are concerned with intellectual, artistic, and personal development.

Know that even if you have great lessons, students—for whatever reason—may not be immediately receptive. That's what years of schooling can do. It emphasizes grades, convergent (read: *closed*) thinking, and conformity, rather than creativity and open-ended thinking. We condition them not to take risks, so they do only what's required. Unfortunately, this mindset is hard to change. You *can*, simply by changing the learning culture in the classroom (see Chapter 10, *Help Students Succeed*).

Action Step

So, use the questions above to write a short paragraph (3–4 sentences) describing your typical student. From there, we can then figure out how best to reach your class. Use the sample paragraph I provided as reference.

Pro Tip: One way to learn more about your students is to come to class early, if possible, and listen to them talk amongst themselves. Here's where you can gain insight into their perspectives—their frustrations and obstacles—often related to other classes. Once, I overheard two students complaining that they never knew what to expect from a certain professor: she provided minimal details about the assignment and students didn't know what they were being tested on. Hearing this strengthened my resolve to manage students' expectations regarding my assignments, something I knew I should be doing but had been shirking. Now, for each assignment, I provide appropriate details and a rubric. Far too many professors walk in minutes before class starts. Even if there is a class before yours, you can wait in the hallway and mingle with your students. Professors strolling in right before class starts are missing a prime opportunity to learn more about their audience—whether by talking to students directly or overhearing conversations.

Consider the Big Picture Goal

The second element to consider is the Big Picture Goal—for your students, *not* your course. Students don't care about your course per se, especially if it is a requirement. Professors sometimes ask students on the first day: "Can anyone tell me why you're all here? Why are you taking this course?" We know how students respond: "Uh, because it's required?" Those questions don't consider the students' perspective.

So forget about your particular course for now. Remember, this first section is about laying the groundwork, so we're staying general at this point.

Instead, ask yourself: *Why are students enrolled in their particular program in the first place?* Planning backward is a strategy that effective educators adopt when planning their day-to-day instruction.[30]

Students are in the school of ed or business school or philosophy program for a reason. You need to be able to state—*in one sentence*—why they're here. This will help you determine what they need.

In my Foundations of Education course, for example, students need to understand all the factors that impact teaching and learning (like class, race, and family). Yet, this course goal is irrelevant to them. Their real, Big Picture Goal is *to become excellent teachers.* For me, then, all they want to learn is how to teach.

Notice I didn't include the following as part of their goal:

- Getting a job (at XYZ Company/Organization)
- Getting an internship
- Passing the XYZ licensing exam (like the CPA, the bar exam, etc.)

All students want these things regardless of the field, so these goals are superfluous. They are short-term goals. Think broader and long term what your students will want to be able to do in their field. Dig deeper into their psychology. What do they *really* want by the time they graduate—other than a job? For my students, it's the ability to teach well and not look bad. If you're still not sure about your students' Big Picture Goal, poll them directly on the first day of class. You can say something like, "Other than a job, what do you hope to get out of this program?" Give them a prompt: *By the time I finish my _____ program, I hope I am able to _____.*

Encourage students to think deeply. They can even discuss in groups or write a short letter to you on the first day (something I've done, to great success). Getting students to think about their goals—particularly those that relate to future careers or aspirations—can help students better prepare or engage with the course.[31]

This will help them *and you* crystallize their Big Picture Goal.

Let's take another example.

If your students are marketing majors, your students' Big Picture Goal might read: *My students enrolled in marketing because they want to go into advertising and be able to develop and create engaging marketing campaigns.*

With certain liberal arts majors, it might be difficult to articulate a Big Picture Goal. But try your best. Think back to when you were in college and what you wanted.

Action Step

So, right now, take five minutes to write a one-sentence statement articulating your students' Big Picture Goal. Here's a prompt to fill in:

My students enroll in _____ *because they want to* _____ *and be able to* _____.

Figure Out the Benefit of Your Course

With the Big Picture Goal in mind, we can now align it to your curriculum goals. What will students gain at the end of the term?

This end result is what marketers call the *benefit*. People, however, often confuse selling a *benefit* with selling a *feature*. For example, saying that telecommunications giant Verizon has the highest Internet connection speed is a *feature*, not a *benefit*. A benefit of fast Internet would be the ability to watch a streaming episode of *Game of Thrones* right now, not later. That's an end result consumers want. We don't care about high Internet connection speed, per se. The benefits of a product or service answer the question: *What's in it for me?* Usually benefits tap into an emotion that people can relate to. Features don't. After all, high-speed Internet sounds good, but what does it do *for me?*

Coca Cola and Apple, among other companies, are masters of figuring out their products' benefits—usually related to an emotion derived from consuming the product. Type in "Apple's Christmas Commercial 2014" on YouTube to see what I mean. I dare you not to cry by the end of this ad. Apple knows their customers value "time spent with Grandma" (a benefit), not high-definition recording (a feature).

Apple holiday commercial 2014 (1:31)

Take my course, Foundations of Education. It's a first-year intro theory course that deals with issues affecting teaching and learning, like race, class, income, and peer group. In this class, my students learn different theories and philosophies of education that give them a broad understanding of teaching and learning. This foundations course is a requirement.

So what is the big benefit? That's not easy to answer, since my course is theory-based and designed mostly to give them foundational knowledge.

I could say the big benefit is: *Students will apply the knowledge from this course to make good teaching decisions.* However, this statement is more about *you* than about them. *You* want them to use the knowledge and apply it, which is fine, but it's not a "client" benefit. What do *they* hope to gain by the end of the semester?

This is why we talked first about the students' Big Picture Goal.

Remember? Let's go back to what I wrote before: *My students enroll in the school of education because they want to become teachers and they want to be able to teach effectively.*

The key is to link your course *benefit* to their Big Picture Goal.

Let's think about it in terms of my foundations course. Their big goal is to be able to teach. You want your students to be able to apply their knowledge to make good teaching decisions. How can we link the two?

How about giving them opportunities to practice teaching? This way, students gain early teaching experience, which helps them reach their goal to teach effectively. They also teach topics relevant to the foundations course, which will help them learn and apply these concepts at a deeper level.

In other words, the big benefit of my course—the reason why students will care—is that:

> *They will get to know what it feels like to teach or feel more confident (by teaching topics related to education foundations), which will prepare them to "student teach" in an elementary classroom during their last year.*

Let's break it down. *They will know what it feels like to teach.* This statement aligns with students' Big Picture Goal of learning how to teach. What student wouldn't want to gain teaching experience as early as possible? The second part—*teaching topics related to education foundations*—relates to my particular course. They will learn a lot about these topics through teaching. The final part—*which will prepare them to student teach during their last year in an elementary classroom*—is another student benefit. They know, even as first-year students, they have to pass student teaching—which is the clinical training portion of their program.

Notice the big benefit is more short term, which makes sense. It is related to your particular course, not students' overall program goal. From this course, they want to gain the competencies, skills, and knowledge that will help them face the next challenge—in this case, student teaching.

Let's take another example, using a writing composition class. What is the students' Big Picture Goal? Again, this is not an easy question to answer when courses are related to the liberal arts. Instead, think about the core interdisciplinary skills and competencies students need for any career.[*] Their Big Picture Goal might be to successfully build their own business or gain the tools needed to succeed in whatever field they go into. Sadly, many students may not know what they want. Again, ask them! What is the big benefit, then, of a writing composition course? Perhaps it is *the ability to move others through the written word.* This may be through cover letters, resumes, blogs, scripts, lyrics, books, etc. If students can see the importance of composition to their world, they

---

[*] While you as the instructor—particularly if teaching a liberal arts course—may see your course as learning for the sake of learning, your students will likely try to connect it to something practical, usually a career. As such, you need to consider *their* expectations for your course—not just yours.

will see utility in your course.

Implications and Action Step

The point of the marketer's mindset is not about "selling" your course or your knowledge. It is about establishing the right mindset in teaching—something most instructors aren't doing. If you cannot think from your students' perspective (including their prior knowledge, their biases, their goals, fears, and obstacles), then the best PowerPoints won't help. Top teachers understand how human beings learn. How? By thinking about how they will help students achieve.[32] Often, this starts by understanding who students are. They won't understand your topic or your course if they come in with weak background knowledge. Foisting your pre-planned lectures will guarantee boredom, resentment, and disengagement. Instead, provide them appropriate and relevant experiences.

Establishing the Big Picture Goal and the benefit for your students is critical for setting the approach and tone of the class, and both should be articulated in your syllabus and your discussions about the course on the first day of class. More about the syllabus in Chapter 4.

Your action step for this chapter is to articulate your students' Big Picture Goal and then a big benefit for your course. Write down two or three different versions. Play around with it and see which makes the most sense. Remember: two instructors teaching the same course will likely have different ideas. The purpose is to articulate to the best of your ability something concrete that can inform your curriculum. This makes all the difference.

So, as we wrap up Chapter 2, remember the marketer's approach: 1) Know your target audience; 2) consider the big picture; and 3) determine the benefit of your service (or, in this case, your course). When you know what students want or need, you can develop a lesson that addresses these factors.

We're also entering the last chapter of Part 1 on laying the groundwork. This new audience-focused mindset will impact the way you develop your lectures and presentations. Without this part, your lectures and lessons cannot improve. In the next chapter, we establish an alternative approach to traditional lectures—an active, hands-on approach.

CHAPTER 3

Adopt an Active Approach

What works for children works just as well for adults.

It took me two years teaching as an adjunct to make this connection. While advertising helped me master consumer psychology, teaching K–12 gave me the nuts and bolts of what worked and didn't work for children. The same applies to undergraduates.

Like children, adults learn best through a hands-on, active approach. While they grasp concepts more abstractly, adults shouldn't have to sit and listen to lectures all class. Research backs this claim. Active learning increases the academic performance of college students, cuts down the failure rate, and reduces the achievement gap between Blacks and whites and between first- and second-generation students.[33] "Learning by doing" is one of the driving forces shaping the next generation of universities.[34]

Yet we tend to think college classrooms *should be* different than those in elementary school. Adults are supposed to be smarter, more mature, and therefore able to sit in forward-facing rows, like they do in auditoriums. Peer instruction expert Eric Mazur disagrees. Desks, he argues, should be set up like elementary school classrooms, where "four children sit around a square table facing each other, and you give them some kind of group activity to work on: that's active learning … that's how we learn. For some reason we unlearn how to learn as we progress from elementary school through middle school and high school."[35]

Often, instructors just assume students are learning. That's what Nobel Laureate Carl Wieman thought in his physics class. When he analyzed students' responses through their handheld electronic clickers, only 10 percent would actually remember the material after twenty minutes of lecture[36]—let alone the next day! "If I'm standing up there talking at them," Wieman surmised, "I have no clue what they're absorbing and not absorbing."[37]

Perhaps you are the same way. You've carefully prepared a PowerPoint lecture. You've included discussion questions. Students appear to be involved. Perhaps you've been blessed with "presence." Yet I hear professors who confess they feel *something* is still lacking; that students may be engaged, but not necessarily learning. I know what they mean—I was one of them. No matter how carefully I planned, I received the same student comments semester after semester: *I wish there were more hands-on practice.*

That was the problem. I was focused more on *teaching* than on helping students *learn*—what students actually *do* in the classroom.

Active learners, according to *Harvard Magazine*, are able to

> *... take new information and apply it, rather than merely taking note of it. Firsthand use of new material develops personal ownership. When subject matter connects directly with students' experiences, projects, and goals, they care more about the materials they seek to master.*[38]

Think of active learning this way: students are *constructing* their own knowledge,[39] rather than receiving it. Class time is used to connect pieces of information—to make sense of it—not to rehash the reading. Professors, therefore, convey much more than knowledge.

They create meaningful experiences.

Active learning seems antithetical in many ways—particularly those in technical fields such as science, technology, engineering, and mathematics (STEM). Covering factual knowledge, after all, is important when there are so many technical details, concepts, and terms. Furthermore, instructors want to set a high bar. They feel they are "gatekeepers" of their profession. Sometimes, these instructors take pride in giving few, if any, A's. Most students, they believe, can't think at a high level and need to be screened out.

I get it. It's tempting to fail certain students for the good of the greater society. In the end, however, it is not our job to determine students' fitness. It is up to the system (or the market)—i.e., college requirements (e.g., GPA, course load) and professional licensure exams (e.g., the bar exam for law, the CPA for accounting, the license exams for teaching). In other words, it is bigger than you. Your job is to get them ready to the best of your abilities, by taking them from Point A to Point B via experiences. That gray area in-between—what psychologist Lev Vygotsky called the *zone of proximal development*—is where you guide them, through the experiences you design (see below).

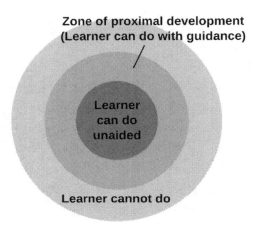

For example, one strategy to help students solve problems is to model a *think aloud session*, which involves narrating how you as the instructor might approach a problem, to help students solve problems on their own: "Hmm, when I see this problem, the first thing I'm thinking is, What do I know so far?" The *think aloud* takes place in the zone of proximal development to "scaffold" student learning. It acts as a model.

Two Approaches to Teaching: "I, We, You" vs. "You, Y'all, We"

One concrete way to see the difference between traditional lectures and active learning is through the *I, We, You* and the *You,*

Y'all, We instructional paradigm. Both are used in K–12 classrooms.

The *I, We, You* paradigm is the more traditional way to teach. First, the instructor does it (*I*). Then, the class does it (*We*). Finally, the individual student does it (*You*). To simplify, here's what it looks like at the elementary school level:

I: *Today, I'm going to show you how to add fractions with different denominators.* (Teacher teaches a strategy.)

We: *Now, let's try a sample problem together.* (Students try another problem with the teacher's guidance—i.e., *guided practice*.)

You: *OK, now that you know how, you can practice more problems in the worksheet!* (Students practice the strategy on their own.)

Sound familiar? That's how most of us learned back in the day. In college classrooms, the *We* typically describes the class discussion and the *You* is where students apply the learning on their own—in their research paper or on the test. The *I, We, You* approach can be useful, however, when students require more teacher guidance or when problems involve complex mathematical steps, like the following engineering question:

A rocket is projected vertically upward and achieves a burnout time equal to zero. It reaches a height above burnout equal to h at time t_1 going up and t_2 coming down. Find h and the speed v_0 at burnout.

Neglect the air drag.

When students encounter this problem for the first time, the instructor may need to clarify the steps by modeling his or her approach. In many STEM-type courses, *I, We, You* approaches may be necessary. However, the downside is that it facilitates linear and inflexible thinking. Often, it leads students to memorize steps rather than think outside the box.

Modeling a strategy has its uses, but I advocate approaches that push nonlinear thinking whenever possible, like the next method called *You, Y'all, We*. It is often credited to math pedagogy scholar Magdalene Lampert.[40]

With the *You, Y'all, We* approach, instructors act more as a guide. Here, the teacher presents a dilemma or situation for students to grapple with individually (the *You*). This allows them to think first without peer influence. They then work together in pairs or groups to come up with a solution or explanation (*Y'all*). Finally, the teacher brings the class together to share and discuss their answers and reasoning (*We*). At this point, the instructor may decide to lecture, if at all. Authentic tasks that arouse student curiosity up front, where students can try, fail, receive feedback, and try again, are critical to in-depth learning.[41]

Let's examine how professors have adopted this active, problem-based approach. In her intro physiology course, neuroscientist Sarah Leupen starts by presenting a problem for students to wrestle with. Instead of merely asking students to name the sensory nerves of the leg, for example, she poses the following:

You're innocently walking down the street when aliens zap away the sensory neurons in your legs. What happens?

a) Your walking movements show no significant change.
b) You can no longer walk.
c) You can walk, but the pace changes.
d) You can walk, but clumsily.

Students then debate the answer, which cannot easily be deduced from factual sources like a textbook. They have to apply what they have learned and argue over options within their group. That struggle is how students learn. Eventually, Leupen explains the right answer (in this case, *d*).

What happens if students get it wrong? "That's usually a good thing," Leupen says, "because then they really remember it."[42] Compare this lesson with one where the instructor spends all class lecturing about the various muscle groups and joints in excruciating detail before testing students.

NPR describes what Stanford physicist Carl Wieman does in his introductory quantum mechanics class:

He starts the class with some slides. "We've talked about how to get even one wave packet like that if we just have a single value momentum," Wieman says, offering up a kind of mini-lecture.

But Wieman quickly switches to giving these undergraduate physics majors a problem to discuss and think about in small groups of four or five.

As students talk through the problem, he walks around the room, just listening in on conversations. He chimes in if a group seems stuck.

"OK, so you can think about how you might produce something like that?" he tells one group. "That's your challenge."

Wieman sees himself as a kind of cognitive coach rather than the classic "sage on the stage," delivering knowledge. His lecturing, such as it is, is merely to prime the undergrads to grapple with the concepts and key questions on their own and try to figure out what's important—or not.

"I'm doing my best to understand what's going on in every one of those students' minds and challenge them and monitor how they're learning," Wieman says. "If I'm just lecturing the whole time, what a terrible waste that would be. Half the material would be over their head and half the material would be completely trivial to them."[43]

Notice how the struggle is what makes students engage, think, and learn. This "problem-based learning" approach helps students develop the collective skills at acquiring, communicating, and integrating information that mirrors (and fosters) twenty-first century work.[44] Science educator Robert Yager likened this process to journalism, where journalists investigate phenomena by finding and querying multiple and credible resources, digesting the information, and summarizing the information in ways that the general public can understand.[45]

The point is to present a problem, a dilemma, or a situation related to the topic (or concept) you want to teach—*rather than teaching it first.* When students work out an issue, they are internalizing the topic in ways that didactic instruction cannot. Only after making sense of the issue, in the students' minds, should the teacher lecture about it. The lecture comes at the end.

Think about it. How do we get young children to play the piano or baseball? We let them tinkle the ivory or give them a ball. The rules and the strategies come later, after children have had a chance to feel it out. We may even teach them specifics at the same time as the play, but what we won't do is sit them down and say, "OK, this is the pitcher's mound. This is the outfield." None of it is relevant or appropriate until after children have had a chance to interact with the ball. Keys like *E flat* or *E natural* mean nothing to the uninitiated. Better to let them explore and then give them guidance and support when appropriate. That's when lecturing can help. In fact, "teaching by telling" works extremely well *after* students have grappled with issues on their own.[46] That's why the "We" in *You, Y'all, We* comes last. The traditional lecture is flipped.

Even if your course isn't problem-based, you can still pose questions. In one of my intro theory courses, students learn basic information about the teaching profession such as salaries, public perception, and its challenges. There is no clear "problem" for students to wrestle with—just factual, foundational knowledge they need to know.

Or is there?

Instead of a PowerPoint detailing the in's and out's of teaching (something I used to do), we must activate students' prior knowledge and perceptions, as done in the following:

> "Today, I want you to think about the field of teaching. I'm interested in what you know or think you know and your perceptions: How much do you think teachers make? How do you think about teaching?"

Imagine a student-led discussion that draws on their assumptions. Students start thinking about what they've heard and read about. Students begin to question their understanding of what it means to be a teacher. Your PowerPoint—if you choose to have one—can easily come at the end, rather than the beginning. Now its sole purpose is not to teach the entire course, but to clarify any ambiguities.

That's how the best K–12 classrooms look. Math education professor Jo Boaler once observed a high school teacher teaching the volume of a complex shape using integrals. But instead of teaching the method first, the teacher asked students to work out a way to find the volume of a lemon—using a knife and a real lemon.

> *After groups had discussed the problem, different students came to the board to excitedly share their ideas. One group had decided to plunge the lemon into a bowl of water to measure the displacement of the*

water. Another had decided to carefully measure the size of the lemon. A third had decided to cut the lemon into thin slices and think of the slices as two-dimensional sections, which they divided into strips, getting close to the formal method for finding the area under a curve that is taught in calculus.

When the teacher explained to students the method of using integrals, they were excited and saw the method as a powerful tool.[47]

These students learned trigonometry methods after grappling with a problem and encountering the need for a method. Only then do the students see formulas and methods as useful—not before, when they are out of context.

Have you ever tried to "pre-teach" vocabulary terms at the beginning of the lecture? In isolation, these words hold no meaning to students. "The [top] professors we studied assumed that learning facts can occur when students are simultaneously engaged in reasoning about those facts," Ken Bain argues in his book, *What the Best College Teachers Do.* This explains why one psychology professor decided to have her students analyze her sanity as a way to understand the label of mental illness—rather than "teach" it. It was her best lesson ever.[48]

This runs counter to the traditional *I, We, You* method where teachers frequently demonstrate the formula or method. Yet, the very struggle students go through to make sense of a problem is precisely the experience that helps them internalize the course content.

College students require hands-on concrete experiences where they have to struggle, or a process of "expectation failure"[49]—when students realize their extant ways of knowing won't serve them adequately—to make sense of a given problem. When we let them do it, students gain so much more.

There is nothing inherently wrong with the traditional *I, We, You* approach to teaching and learning. Students can still benefit, as long as there is active involvement. There might be certain courses or topics that require a teacher demonstration or modeling—where students get a chance to struggle with a similar experience afterward. Often, fields like chemistry and other STEM fields require the expert to *show* first.

You, as the instructor, must make that decision about what works best for your course and each class. Students might benefit from struggling with a concept first in one class, whereas they might be better served if you show them something in another class. Chapter 7, *Craft the Lesson*, will provide a template for both kinds of lessons.

Conclusion and Action Steps

What you've read in Part 1 lays the groundwork for great teaching, which I argue is about students, not you. If you want to stop students from texting or daydreaming, then start by thinking from their perspective—their needs, wants, fears, and passions (what I call a *marketer's mindset*). This includes reflecting on your course goals, the Big Picture Goal, and the big benefit of your course for students. These end goals crystallize the foundation of helping students learn and propel you into the next part of the book, where we develop your lesson/presentation.

At this point, I want you to think about how you have been teaching your course. Have you relied on slides? How can a *You, Y'all, We* approach to teaching and learning be used in your classroom? Jot down ways students can actively grapple with problems, rather than listen to lectures.

In Part 2, *Plan Your Lesson*, we get into the nitty-gritty, revamping your syllabus to stimulate student interest (Chapter 4), *niching* your topic (Chapter 5), engaging your audience (Chapter 6), and crafting a lesson outline (Chapter 7).

PART 2

Plan Your Lessons

CHAPTER 4

Start with Your Syllabus

Imagine you find yourself in one of the following scenarios:

Scenario 1:

It's August 20th. Let's see ... I have one week before classes start and three courses to teach. Time to update last spring's syllabi. I should probably insert some new articles. Maybe revise the course policies. Last semester, too many students didn't do the reading, so something needs to change. Maybe give them a quiz every class? Find better texts? I also need to enforce the attendance policy better—too many students just waltzed in halfway through my lecture. I wonder what Google has to say about that?

Scenario 2:

It's August 25th. I can't believe the university just offered me a course to teach last minute—c'mon, guys, where's my time to plan? I don't even have a university email address! Well, at least I have a syllabus

from the last instructor. Even better, they emailed me a digital copy.
I'll use her texts, her course policies and assignments, and then I'll
improve on it as I go along.

As an adjunct professor, I've experienced both scenarios. Either
way, I didn't spend enough time developing my syllabi. Most of us
follow a template and rarely question it. Because of that, we're not
thinking about the student perspective. Is it a coincidence that
syllabi are increasingly viewed as contracts—dense, detached, and
unreadable? But they are not. Contracts are terms of expectations
that both parties can agree to and sign—neither of which students
do. In reality, it is used to cover the asses of those who write them.

This chapter shows you *how* to write your syllabus, as opposed to
what to write. If you want the latter, I recommend Clair Johnson's
article, "Best Practices in Syllabus Writing: Contents of a Learner-
Centered Syllabus," which offers a clear breakdown and includes a
free, downloadable checklist (see the resources list at the end of this
book).[50] Much more important, however, is your mindset, as
Chapter 2 (*Focus on Your Student, Not the Content*) alluded to. Let's
start by establishing the right way to see the syllabus.

The Syllabus as a Communication Piece

I once attended a workshop on writing effective grant proposals
given by the National Science Foundation (NSF). Hearing the
reality from the reviewers' perspective was eye opening.

They all seemed to say the same thing: *clear communication*
matters.

One reviewer summed it up this way:

Imagine that you've submitted a proposal to NIH [National Institutes of Health]. Your reviewer is reading through the proposals, but she's left at the last moment. It's 6 a.m. on the day she's flying to Washington. She's sitting at the bus stop, it's raining, she has the flu, and she's got your proposal in front of her. Your writing should be able to persuade her that this is a great proposal, even under those conditions.[51]

Reviewers simply have too many complex proposals to review in a very short period of time.

"I wish I had a better sense of the time frame so that I could have done a better job clearing my plate in the week that I had to read proposals," wrote one former NSF reviewer.[52]

Another reviewer wrote about the importance of getting to the big picture early on: "I used to just plod through each proposal, focusing on all the details … Now I get to the gestalt, the big picture first. If I like it, then I'll go on to the details. If I don't, I'm done reading."[53]

We as researchers don't realize how much poor communication undermines our chances of being selected.

If reviewers, with their scholarly pedigrees, require a "simpler, livelier writing style"[54] to continue reading, then students need it even more. As instructors, we have to know our students before crafting our course, our syllabus, or our lesson. This *marketer's mindset* is critical and explains why it is one of this book's major recurring themes.

Think of it from the perspective of students. They aren't choosing to take your course, per se. Even if it's an elective, students don't really know what kind of instructor they're getting.

Will the professor be nice?

Will this course be useful?

It's not like choosing a book on Amazon, where you can read the description, reviews, and details beforehand.[*]

So skepticism is the real obstacle you must overcome. Students want to know their time isn't being wasted. They're being rational.

That's why we need to rethink the syllabus. It needs to reassure them yet inspire, as communication professor Curtis Newbold argues:

> *Shouldn't a syllabus get a student excited about learning? Shouldn't it empower a student to embrace the content and the challenge? Shouldn't it clarify and communicate? Shouldn't it answer what the students want to know? Students are paying for the course, after all. Isn't it about them? Certainly.*[55]

In the end, the syllabus is a communication piece.[†] Treat it like a

---

[*] While students can read reviews on sites like RateMyProfessor.com, most are still stuck with few options, particularly if the course is required. As such, these sites function more to preview students will face and less to provide choices.

[†] Habanek (2005), for instance, describes the function of the syllabus as "a major communication device that provides details of how student learning will be

sales brochure or a motivational speech, not a contract. Maybe we can't remove certain language content (e.g., policies and requirements), but we can use it to build relationships. That's what effective communication does. It's a lesson from marketing we can apply to higher education.

Start with the Big Picture Questions

If you search online for the major elements of a syllabus, most sources will include something like the following:

- Contact info
- Course details (date/time, room, course section number, etc.)
- Course description
- Course prerequisites
- Objectives/outcomes
- Course policies (attendance, behavior, how to submit assignments, etc.)
- Required texts
- Course rubrics/breakdown of assignments (e.g., participation is worth 10%)
- Course calendar (details what you will do each class)
- Required language on academic integrity and disability services

---

assessed and about the roles of both student and instructors in the learning and assessment process."

Although all syllabi include these elements, they rarely answer the *why* and the *how*. But this rationale is necessary: *Why do students need to take this course? Why are these assignments necessary? How does it fit into their future career? How will this course help them* [get a job]? These are the questions students care about. Answer these big picture questions in the syllabus.

For example, my students don't necessarily realize why they must take a foundational course in education. My syllabus, therefore, tells them that as future educators, they need to know all the factors that affect teaching and learning, such as motivation, class, family, and popular culture. In my child development course, I actually make the big picture question the final paper question: *How do you develop children into successful adults?* While broad, it makes the purpose of the course explicit. Students know from day one what they are striving to answer. Walk into my child development class any random week and ask them, "What's your finals question?" My students will tell you.

Furthermore, knowing the big picture helps teachers align their assignments and lessons with the course objectives through backward design.[56] On a practical level, thinking broadly can help instructors link their units, topics, and readings coherently, as well as pace their lessons appropriately.

Here are some other oft-neglected questions to consider:[57]

1. How does the course make a difference as part of the discipline? How does it fit into the general-education

program?

2. Why do the parts of the course come in the order that they do?

3. Will the course be primarily lectures, discussions, or group work?

4. What will the tests be testing? Memory? Understanding? Ability to synthesize, present evidence logically, apply knowledge in a new context?

5. Why have the books been chosen? What is their relative importance in the course and in the discipline? Is the emphasis on primary or secondary materials, and why?

Students will find the syllabus useful when professors think through such questions. They don't care about course objectives and outcomes, which, although important, are for accreditation purposes anyway.[*] They want a syllabus that suggests accessibility, warmth, and utility. Unfortunately, most faculty (including me) learned to write syllabi by mimicking colleagues. Starting with the big-picture

---

[*] Many departments require that faculty use a syllabus template or put in certain language as a way to prevent academic and legal disputes with students. It's unfortunate. I will say, as much as possible, talk to your chair and show them the alternative—one you wrote that is reader friendly but at the same time mirrors the contents of the required elements; after all, there should be consistency with course bulletins and other policy documents. Student learning objectives and other language are important, especially when they are linked to school accreditation.

questions is the first step to creating a learner-centered syllabus.

You can answer many of these questions in the course description. Ask yourself, *What is this course really about?* Economics professor Lolita Paff shows one way how:[58]

Course Description

Before	After
Econ102 is an introduction to microeconomic analyses and policies. Microeconomic deals with the behavior of individuals and firms and how the behavior is influenced by government policy. The principal objective of the course is to enable students to analyze major microeconomic issues clearly and critically.	Why should you want to study microeconomics? Alfred Marshall defined economics as the study of people in the ordinary business of life. Every choice you make—from what time to get up, whether or not to go to class, how long to study or work, or how much to eat, or where to go on Thursday nights—ALL of it incorporates microeconomic principles. Microeconomics helps us to understand how people and firms make choices, how markets are organized, why and how markets behave differently, and the effects government interventions have in market outcomes. I LOVE this course, and I am hoping that by the end of the semester you will develop a deep appreciation for the subject.

Notice she didn't title this section "Course Description." Instead, she asks, *Why should you want to study microeconomics?* Writing headings as questions is an old trick web designers use to make webpages easier to read.[59] Professor Curtis Newbold did the same in a business communication course:

In an ultra-competitive, brand-focused, media-conscious, digitally active world, organizations need business communicators who understand that design is as persuasive as content; that search engines tell consumers what is credible; and that interactivity isn't just a trend, it's a fundamental component of a client's experience. As a communication professional, you live in an age where creativity, flexibility, and adaptability often trump the standards of old. It's time to take the best practices of the past and mold them to where the future is headed.[60]

Newbold treats his students as professionals. Imagine how differently it sounds compared to: "In this course, students will learn the fundamentals of business communication in a digital society…"

Simply uninspiring.

My child development course description challenges students' pre-existing notions of educating children:

Why is this course important?
Did you know that telling a child he or she is "smart" is not such a good idea? That listening to adults talk is not necessarily the best way for young children to learn? That "failing" can actually be a good

thing? This course helps you better understand the young learner and how to develop them into successful adults.

These questions intrigue. Think how your course might arouse a student's curiosity. Each of the following questions does so, for various disciplines:

What makes a good teacher? (education)

How does your brain work? (human development)

What is the nature of justice? (law, philosophy)

How do we know what we know? (epistemology)

Why are some people rich and some poor? (sociology)

How do you get others to see your point of view? (communication)

All course descriptions ought to *provoke* while still communicating what the course is about. Again, think of it like the opening paragraph of your cover letter, your sales brochure, or your book. It has to "hook" the reader.

 Pro Tip: When you change the language of certain boilerplate elements like academic integrity and course objectives, you should have an administrator like the department chair review it, particularly if this is your first year at the institution. They may require strict adherence.

Optimizing the Language

Aside from inspiring and reassuring skeptical students, a syllabus also says a lot about how you run the class and how you see your students. It's why experts recommend writing syllabi in a more friendly, approachable tone.[61]

This means using positive, rewarding language versus those that are punishing (i.e., the ones that are boldfaced or all caps that demonstrate harsh consequences). A friendly, approachable tone also means providing a rationale for assignments and policies—a *why*—and showing enthusiasm.

Revise the boilerplate language used by the department (insofar as you have the authority to do so) to make it reader friendly. Often, this means talking *to* students rather than *at* them. One way is to replace the word *student* with *you* (the second-person voice). Compare, for instance, the official language of my course with my own version:

Less Reader-Friendly Language	More Reader-Friendly Language
Course Outcomes • Candidates will develop an understanding of the essential issues of child development in various cultural contexts and be able to explain theoretical materials reviewed in class and apply these materials to their	What should you be able to *know* and *do* by the end of this course? • You will develop an understanding of the essential issues of child development in various cultural contexts. • You will be able to explain theoretical materials and

observations of children in classrooms. • Candidates will read chapters and articles and will critique each reading through journal entries and class discussions. In addition, each student will teach/present one of the readings and engage the class. • Candidates will observe the behavior and learning of children in various classroom contexts and at different phases of development and will learn ways to describe and understand these behaviors during their fieldwork.	apply them to your observations of children in the classroom. • You will be able to teach or lead a lesson on a given topic. • You will be able to describe and understand children's behavior and learning in various classroom contexts and at different phases of development.

You might think the outcomes on the left are just as easy to understand. The half-distracted, weary student would disagree. Think back to the sick NIH reviewer sitting in the rain, reading your proposal. Remember, the syllabus is written for *them*, not for you. Think the same way when you present your course policies and other sections.

It is crucial that you get into the habit of using *positive* or at least *neutral* language. Terms like "do not" (as in, "DO NOT use cell phones") assume the worst in people, while phrases like "will result in failure" (as in, "Three absences will result in course FAILURE") sound overly alarming. Frequent use of boldface and all caps will also tire quickly. Instead, reframe sentences as suggestions or advice, *along with a rationale.*[62]

Instead of writing:	Write this:
DO NOT use cell phones in class … or The use of cell phones (including texting) is strictly prohibited in class.	Avoid using cell phones in class, which can prevent you or others from learning. In cases of emergency, please take your phone outside.
Students must notify the instructor of accommodations within 2 weeks of class.	If you need accommodations, let me know as soon as possible. You have the right to have your needs met.
You must complete makeup work to receive credit.	You are welcome to make up missed work to earn credit.
I only accept papers that are …	I encourage you to submit papers that …
Late work will result in a 40% deduction	If your work is late, you can still qualify for 60% of the original points.

Students may argue, "But you said we're 'encouraged' to submit papers that are double-spaced, not that it's required!" So providing a rationale is important:

I encourage you to submit papers that are written in twelve-point type size, double-spaced, with one-inch margins. These are industry standards. Using double-space allows me room to give you better feedback.

If they don't adhere to it, then just let it be.[*] If, however, these incidents happen regularly, consider them issues of class citizenship and behavior, rather than points to be deducted on an assignment. Talk to the individual or the class as a teachable moment. Is there a reason for their noncompliance? What kind of an impression does it leave when students refuse to comply? In the end, it may not be worth it. Forcing compliance—and then penalizing students when they don't comply—rarely changes behavior. It's better to treat them as capable adults and expect they will make the right decisions. The language used reflects your perspective of students as mature, responsible adults.

Better yet, cultivate an engaging, positive, safe classroom that minimizes deviance.

 Pro Tip: Always print out hardcopies of the syllabus for your students *and* put them online—not just one or the other. With hardcopies, students can mark them up and bring them to class. Online versions of the syllabus rarely get read all the way through (online courses are a different matter). But students can always reprint them

---

[*] That is, of course, unless you have a reason for taking off points; e.g., it is an English writing course.

when necessary. Furthermore, those who miss the first day can catch up with an online syllabus.

Ten Pro Tips for Writing a Syllabus

1. Use active voice whenever possible. It makes your syllabus clearer, more personal, and collaborative,[63] and less like a research paper or contract: *I encourage you to …* versus *Students are encouraged to …*

2. To maintain flexibility and avoid overwhelming students, keep the syllabus short (the average length is 7.4 pages[64]). Shorter syllabi will be read. I also adhere to the "just-in-time" approach used in inventory management to provide details: elements like rubrics and assignment details are provided as needed.

3. Consider using alternate, visually appealing formats (see next section).

4. If you're required to keep certain language word-for-word (including those for academic integrity and course objectives), put them in the back of the syllabus—in small fine print if necessary. Or put them online. Reserve the front for the syllabus that students will read.*

5. Consider sharing information about yourself, which can warm relationships (think how profiles are used in blogs or social media

---

* Asking you to put course info in the back may be controversial. That's why I argue to modify the language as a first alternative. In the end, whose interests are we serving?

sites like LinkedIn).

6. Provide useful suggestions (e.g., What's the best way to take notes? Where can students get extra help? What's the best way to stay on track or attack complicated assignments? What does a typical class look like? What are useful websites for more information? How quickly do you return submitted assignments or email questions? What are some common misconceptions about your discipline/course?). I put these as sidebar text boxes to draw attention and break the syllabus up visually.

7. Make due dates more accessible by repeating them throughout the syllabus. For example, I put due dates not only in the course calendar, but also the sections detailing course assignment and grading scale.

8. If relevant, consider structuring your course syllabus by ideas or experiences (e.g., race, class, gender) rather than by book sections (e.g., chapter 1, chapter 2). (See Chapter 5, *Develop Your Topic*, for more about this approach.)

9. Ask yourself if each assignment actually has a purpose—does it reflect your course objectives/outcomes and will students see its utility? Or does it actually just keep students busy? (e.g., why are students writing text responses—is it to build a dialogue with the text or to ensure they do the reading?) If assignments are somewhat vague or unhelpful, take them out.

10. Consider what makes your course/section different from others. In marketing, your *unique selling proposition* (USP) separates your product or service from those of your competitors. TOMS shoes,

for example, donates a new pair of shoes to a child in need for every customer purchase. Domino's Pizza guarantees hot pizza delivered to your door in 30 minutes or less—or it's free. Do you have a novel instructional approach? Do you use more hands-on activities? Do you include proprietary materials? In my math methods course, I give students a "best resources" guide that compiles my list of top teacher planners, books, math apps, websites, and other resources for the future math teacher. Whatever USP(s) you have, include them in your syllabus. It will help you stand out.

Optimizing the Layout and Presentation

Even if you follow the suggestions above, it may not be enough. A well-crafted syllabus should be visually accessible as well. Nobody wants to read big blocks of texts. Professors forget we live in a visual age where Pinterest, emojis, and memes rule. Where *too long; didn't read* (tl;dr) is an actual thing people say in the online community.

Design is not about making the syllabus look good. It is about communicating and solving problems. When done well, good design makes life easier. Have you ever tried to push a door when it should be pulled? Poor design makes life harder. So does a poorly designed syllabus. Most of them look terrible.

For an easy-to-read primer on design principles, read *The Non-Designer's Design Book*, by Robin Williams (no, not the actor).

Why not use a design approach—pictures, quotes, and profiles—to communicate your passion for your discipline? Think of what students read and how pages are designed on smartphones, tablets, and social media sites. I've seen, for instance, visually appealing syllabi that use flow charts and diagrams to show how the readings connect.[65] Microsoft Word and Apple's Pages, among many sources, offer free templates like newsletters you can alter—as I did for my child development course (see the "before" and "after"). You are limited to your imagination. What can you do to communicate your passion about your discipline, course, and students?

For more examples of visually appealing syllabi as well as free downloads, see *The Visual Communication Guy* blog at TheVisualCommunicationGuy.com/course-syllabi.

BEFORE

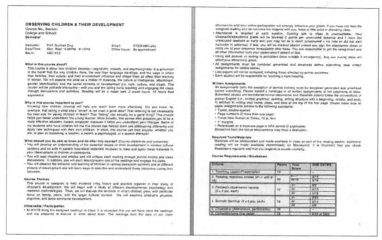

AFTER*

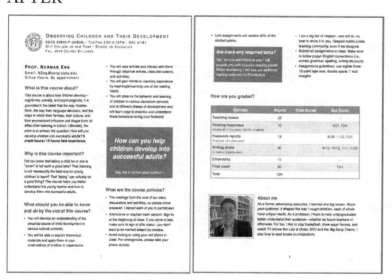

* If you're interested in this exact template, it came from Apple Pages (Version 5.6), called School Newsletter. Also, note that my two-column format makes it easier for students, particularly those with dyslexia and other reading challenges, to read.

Considerations for Visually Appealing Layouts

- Intersperse visuals appropriate for your course (photographs, illustrations, graphic), but be careful not to distract the eye with too many!

- Alternate type sizes to emphasize certain elements like course title and section headings. Be careful, however, not to use too many different sizes, which undermine visual coherence. Try one type size for headings, one size for body, and if necessary one more for others (like fine print and sidebars). This creates visual cohesion and lends clarity.

- Utilize text boxes to call attention to certain areas or for quotes (think how magazines employ sidebars)

- Use at least 1.15 or more for line spacing (rather than single-spaced, which crams texts).

- Note of caution: Be mindful that not all students appreciate excessive colors and visuals, especially when it comes to printing. Offer a black-and-white or simpler version for the budget- or environmentally conscious individual disinclined to wasting ink or paper.

Tulane University's *Accessible Syllabus* has tools to make your syllabus more accessible, inclusive, and engaging—including images and texts. Go to accessiblesyllabus.tulane.edu.

 Pro Tip: To ensure students read the syllabus, allow students five to ten minutes to read it *in class* uninterrupted. For many, this will be the only time they read your syllabus thoroughly. Encourage students to jot notes and questions and then review answers as a class. For large classes, have them break into groups, where students can ask each other questions. This will cut down their questions for you.

I've heard of professors who "quiz" students or play recall activities like the jigsaw[66] to ensure students have read it. A few instructors have even embedded "Easter eggs" or hidden gems (e.g., "If you've made it this far into the syllabus, please email me a picture of a dinosaur"), which invariably catches (many) inattentive students.[67] At least it's humorous. Experiment with these methods and let me know if they work for you.

What If You've Already Handed Out Your Syllabus?

It's hard to alter the syllabus once you've distributed it to students and submitted it to the department. Better to wait for the following semester to revamp it. But do not worry: the approaches and techniques in the following chapters are aimed to improve your lessons regardless. While a big-picture, learner-centered syllabus will help a lot, you can still benefit by modifying your lesson planning (which we will do next chapter).

 Pro Tip: During the course of the semester, I write ongoing notes on the side of my syllabus (e.g., *Move this unit back another week. Replace with new article. Clarify late submission policy*). I even incorporate feedback from the department observations and student evaluations right on the syllabus. This way, when next semester rolls around, all the changes are easy to see.

Action Step

The syllabus is the one document that represents your course and one that students can constantly refer to. As such, it deserves more attention than we give it. Setting the tone—through our approach, our language, and our design—is a part of effective communication. Take this time to rethink the syllabus. What can you do to intrigue students?

Start with the big questions—what is your course about? Then, optimize your language to make your course (and you) more accessible to students. Make it friendly. Finally, consider ways to make it easy to read and absorb, from a visual perspective. Combined, these tactics will ensure your syllabus will be among the top 10 percent of syllabi read by students and considered learner-centered.

Next chapter, we focus on the day-to-day topics; specifically, how you can narrow it and make it relevant to students' lives.

CHAPTER 5

Develop Your Topic

In this chapter, you will rework your topic by:

1. Narrowing in on key areas
2. Generating a lesson objective and essential question
3. Making the topic relevant
4. Search for the underlying idea or universal experience

First off, what do I mean by *topic*? A *topic* is something you want to address within the course of one class session. It could be a concept, a person, an event, or a phenomenon. For example, my topic could be on disciplining children or on Swiss psychologist Jean Piaget, about which students will read a specific article or chapter beforehand. The key, however, is to focus on specific parts of the topic, rather than lecture everything about it. While this is obvious, it is in direct conflict with the imperative to cover the curriculum.

Too many instructors attempt to shoehorn exhaustive content into one topic.

1. Focus on one to three areas of your topic.

People learn more when less is presented.[68] But because we have a lot to cover, we cram. The tradeoff, however, is that students leave the class confused.[69] If you've ever thought, *Wow, today's lecture was productive—I was able to cover so much!*, you've got a problem. Your students are too busy taking notes to listen or remember much.

The best professors and presenters constantly prune the content of their topic.[70] They prefer to inspire attention to important matters rather than be encyclopedic. A laser-like focus facilitates in-depth, critical thinking. It also ensures that audiences leave *remembering*. Therefore, *what* you're presenting/teaching is more important than *how much*: quality over quantity. Focus instead on the ideas that are 1) notable; 2) difficult to learn; 3) rooted in common misperception; and/or 4) fundamental principles in your field.[71]

Let's practice with my foundations course as an example. As mentioned, students here learn about all the things that affect teaching and learning. It's a first-year theory course for education majors.

One topic we focus on regards Paulo Freire, a Brazilian educator. Essentially, he believed in empowering students—especially those without a voice. He felt that traditional education perpetuates the agenda of those in power and silences the voices of minorities. Freire thus called for a "pedagogy of the oppressed." I teach about Freire because my undergraduates need to be sensitive to the voices of their future students.

A whole class devoted to Freire is typical, as professors often build entire courses on a particularly influential figure in their field. However, lecturing about him ("Let's talk about Freire's impact on the field of education ...") will likely bore students who perceive little connection to him. Most will think, *Who is this guy? Who cares about him? Why do I need to know him or his theories?*

The point isn't for students to know everything about Freire or even why he is important. They need to know *how his ideas can help them become better teachers.* That is, after all, how the subject of Freire pertains to the course, and therefore, the students. As such, we as instructors must present the core ideas that make this figure relevant.

First, clarify then simplify what you want to teach. Find one to three things important about your topic, the parts you want your students to walk out of class remembering. I call this *niching down*—or narrowing—your topic.

If you have a long class, maybe you can find three important things. Most typical ninety-minute classes, however, should focus on no more than a couple of major points.*

———————————

* If you find there are simply too many areas of your topic that are important, then chances are that this topic is more a unit, which requires multiple class sessions. For example, "social foundations of education" is too broad to be considered as a topic. Same with "race." I might consider Buddhism or Teaching Whole Numbers a unit that requires several sessions, but it really depends on your course and curriculum.

Continuing with my example, the main idea I want to communicate is Paulo Freire's *banking concept of education*. It refers to the traditional way of schooling, where knowledge is "deposited" into the minds of students to be retrieved later, like money in a bank. According to Freire, one-way instruction is an instrument of oppression, because it treats students as empty vessels rather than active agents of learning. With extra time, I might also address his idea of oppression in education.

Now you have a go. Take your topic and "niche it down" to the essentials. Think about what you really want students to know by the end of each lecture. Then write down your one to three major "essences." My example with Paulo Freire has been provided as reference.

Lesson Topic:	
Sample: Paulo Freire (Brazilian educator)	
Essential Idea #1	*Sample: The banking concept of education, where knowledge is deposited into the minds of students to retrieve later*
Essential Idea #2 (if necessary)	*Sample: Oppression in education, with the teacher as potential oppressor and students as potentially oppressed.*
Essential Idea #3 (if necessary)	*Sample: Education should be more about "problem-posing," which emphasizes critical thinking to liberate the mind.*

2. *Generate your lesson objective and essential question.*

Secondly, what is your lesson objective? This is what you want students to be able to know and do by the end of the class and should be related to your broader course objectives and outcomes. The lesson objective, however, is written *for you*, not for students. More important for students is the essential question, such as, "How can we evaluate the credibility of sources to protect our democracy from the influence of those spreading misinformation?" Not only does it drive the lesson, it triggers interest in a way that lesson objectives do not.

"The lesson objective is written *for you*, not for students. More important for students is the essential question ... Not only does it drive the lesson, it triggers interest in a way that lesson objectives do not."

Regardless, lesson objectives are important. They guide the content and the activities. My generic formula answers *what* they will be able to do and *how*. Here are two ways to say the same objective:

Students will be able to evaluate the credibility of sources [the what] by using the triangulation method [the how].

Students will use the triangulation method [the how] to evaluate the credibility of sources [the what].

 Pro Tip: Make lessons more useful by adding the simple stem "so that" at the end of the objective to describe how the skill or content can benefit students:[72]

Objective: Students will be able to evaluate the credibility of sources by using the triangulation method so that they can protect our democracy from the influence of those spreading misinformation.

Create a lesson objective from one of your class topics.

Topic:

Sample: Researching social studies topics

Lesson Objective:

What will they be able to do? *Students will ...*
How will they accomplish this? *By ...*
How does this benefit them? *So that ...*

Sample: Students will be able to evaluate the credibility of sources by using the triangulation method.

---

3. Make it relevant!

With Paulo Freire as my topic, I have an essential idea to teach: the *banking concept of education.* The next step is to make that concept concrete. How? Ask yourself the following three questions (I've provided sample answers as reference):

Question	Sample Answer	Your Answer (Based on your topic)
Why is this idea important or meaningful?	*Freire's banking concept of education characterizes one of the least effective ways to teach, and therefore we should avoid this approach.*	
How can you make this idea easier to understand?	*1. I could tell a personal story about falling asleep regularly during an accounting course.* *2. I could ask students about their past experiences with traditional lectures.* *3. I could deconstruct the banking metaphor.*	
How can students apply this idea?	*Have students brainstorm two ways to teach, for example, pizza- making: through the "banking concept" approach (i.e., traditional lecture) followed by a more "active" way (e.g., demonstration).*	

Answering these three questions helps you generate an essential question. You can establish one from your niched concept. The essential question should focus on important, transferable ideas within (and sometimes across) disciplines.[73] This means relating it to students' lives or the larger society they live in.

In my case, here's how I might frame Freire's banking concept as an essential, relevant question:

How can Paulo Freire's "banking concept of education" help you engage your future students?

Notice how I took a potentially dry concept (*banking concept of education*) and made it meaningful. This guiding question aligns with my big course benefit (giving students exposure to teaching through foundational issues) and aligns with their Big Picture Goal (learning how to teach). Here are three formats to guide your essential question:

How can [insert your niche concept/idea here] *help you* [insert desired outcome]?

Why is [insert your niche concept/idea here] *an important part of* [insert a competency or skill]?

Why is [insert your niche concept/idea here] *important for* [insert students' potential career]?

Here are some more examples, using different course disciplines:

- How can *the theory of multiple intelligences* help you *design a lesson that considers children's strength modalities?*
- Why is *social media marketing* an important part of *an effective marketing campaign?*

- How can *using the active voice* help you *make your writing more persuasive?*

Now write down one essential question and make sure it incorporates an element that relates to your students as professionals.

4. Search for the underlying idea or universal experience.

Another way to make your topic relevant is to search for the underlying idea or human experience. What do I mean?

Let's take some typical course content: Rousseau. Skinner. The Gettysburg Address. The central nervous system. Covalent bonding. Shintoism. Consumer branding.

These are the *content* students have to know. But you shouldn't start your lesson teaching content by saying:

"Today, we're going to delve into the reading on B.F. Skinner and how his theory on *operant conditioning* shaped modern psychology."

It sounds like a typical opening. But it's wrong. Why? Because Skinner's theory doesn't mean anything to students, at least in the beginning. To make content meaningful, instructors should start with the underlying human experience. For instance, K–12 teachers know that topics in math, for instance, should relate to real life. So they ask children about their experiences with money before teaching them about it.

Let's look for the underlying experience behind Skinner's theory on operant conditioning. First, a quick refresher: Skinner's theory on operant conditioning states that when behavior is reinforced, it is strengthened. When it is not reinforced, people stop doing the behavior. For example, a teenage boy will probably eat more pizza if he is surrounded by his male friends, all of whom want to show off how much they can "wolf down." On the other hand, he will likely stop eating so much if he is surrounded by his family, who care about his wellbeing and may encourage him to eat more healthily.

Using Skinner's concept of operant conditioning, a professor might define the universal experience or fundamental idea undergirding the concept. What if, for instance, she started the lesson this way:

"Today, I want you to think of a time when you were punished for something you did—either at home or at school, or with friends."

[Pause.]

"Go ahead, think of something. It might be for going out when you were supposed to be studying; it might be for bullying, or even for wearing clothes your parents disapproved of. Maybe your friends gave you the cold shoulder for something you did. Come up with one experience where you were 'punished' in some way."

The professor could have easily asked students to think about a time they were rewarded as well. The point is to put students into a situation they can relate to and tap into a universal feeling, idea, or experience that engages them at a personal level.

Only after students make sense of their experiences should the instructor bring up the term *operant conditioning* or the psychologist behind the concept, B. F. Skinner. This professor might then say:

"Did you continue to do these behaviors? Why or why not?" [Have a short discussion on why we modify our behavior when we are negatively or positively reinforced]

She can then bring up the idea of operant conditioning and Skinner's experiments with caged rats, where they were "conditioned" to press a lever to receive food pellets. By then, students will see a connection and internalize the idea of rewards and punishments through their prior experiences. All because she gave them *context*. Research shows we learn new things within the context of what we know.[74]

Granted, looking for the experience behind the content may be more difficult in disciplines like chemistry or physiology. If that's the case, try to find the underlying *idea*. In math, for instance, the underlying idea behind the concept of *slope* is steepness. How can one make that concrete to students?

To simplify, let's explore how a second grade math teacher might help students understand the universal experience or underlying idea behind fractions.

"Class, I have three chocolate bars. But let's say there are four of you, and you want to share these three bars equally. How would you do that?"

[Pause.]

"Let's figure it out. Why don't you all get into groups of four and try it out?"

Notice how the teacher hasn't even brought up the word *fractions*, hasn't used words like *numerator* and *denominator*, hasn't instructed the students to shade in rectangles on worksheets—all of which was standard procedure when we were young. Children won't relate to worksheets and abstract concepts when encountering fractions for the first time. We forget what that felt like (the so-called *expert blind spot*). Why else would so many adults, especially those who are American, hate math?[*]

Having students share bars, through trial and error, taps into the

---

[*] I'm reminded of the burger wars in the 1980s when the A&W restaurant chain released a new hamburger to rival McDonald's famous Quarter Pounder. While it was tastier and bigger—at a third of a pound of beef, A&W's burger fared poorly. The reason? Customers thought they were getting a raw deal—"Why would we pay the same for less beef?" They thought one-third was less than one-quarter—a monumental math fail. These adults probably learned fractions in very abstract and confusing ways.

universal experience of children—namely, being fair. Only after they "struggle with" or make sense of the situation will the teacher then bring up mathematical terms like *numerator* and *denominator*. Only then will children see the relationship between their experiences and the content. And chances are, now that they have that context, they will remember it.

Once, I observed one of my students teaching bar graphs to a group of first graders. Bar graphs are an important concept that children need to know, right? Yet here's how she started the lesson:

"Good morning class. Has anyone ever heard of a *bar graph*?" [A few children nod.]

"Great! What do you know about them?" [A couple of students attempt to answer the question, but the answers are generally off base.]

"That's OK, because today we're going to learn what a *bar graph* is and how to make one. OK?"

[Pause.]

"First, we start with the *title*. What should we call it? Why don't we call it *Favorite Ice Cream Flavors*? OK. Then we need *labels* on the bottom of the table with the names of our favorite flavors, like vanilla, chocolate, and strawberry ..."

You see the problem? This student was trying to teach the *content* first—with all its requisite terms like *title* and *label*. This is the classic

I, We, You approach mentioned in Chapter 3, which focuses on teacher-directed instruction. While serviceable, this method strips the essence—the idea—behind bar charts (i.e., capturing information we care about) and reduces it to a meaningless abstraction. Children remain passive when the steps are prescribed, even if engaging questions are sprinkled throughout.

Instead, this teacher should look for the *idea* behind bar graphs: *What are bar graphs actually for? Why—and when—are they useful?* Imagine starting a lesson this way:

"Class, I think strawberry is the favorite ice cream flavor of the class. You agree, no?"

Children: "No!!!" [Children are often quick to prove their teacher wrong.]

"Well, what is the favorite?"

[Students give various answers.]

"That's a lot of different answers. I wonder which one the class favors the most? We should find out. How do you think we should do that?"

[Ask children how they want to find out—by raising hands?

Secret ballot? Voting with their feet?*]

"OK, now we need to find a way to *show* how students voted. How can we do that?"

[Students offer ideas.]

"One way to do this is by showing it as a picture. We call it a *bar graph* ..."

Do you see where this is going? While the name of the concept (*bar graph*) matters, the idea behind it is even more important. The teacher has challenged the students to investigate what flavor the class prefers. Isn't that the idea behind bar graphs—to capture group data and represent it visually? Students will see the relevance of bar graphs as they work toward finding out the truth! Terms like *x-axis*, *y-axis*, and *key* will come as a natural part of learning, rather than forced, seemingly arbitrary concepts. This will help students understand concepts more deeply.

Psychologist Jean Piaget once said, "When you teach a child something, you take away forever his chance to discover it himself." *Start with the experience; then relate it to the content.*

––––––––––––––––––––

* The expression "voting with your feet" refers to your ability to "walk" to situations you believe to be more beneficial or leave those you do not like. In a classroom context, this typically involves students walking to a different area of the room, each of which represents their vote ("Go to Corner A if you strongly agree; go to Corner B if you strongly disagree ...").

"Start with the experience; then relate it to the content."

What are the topics you teach? Think about the content students need to know—the people, the theories, the concepts—and then think about the *experiences* or *ideas* that underscore them. To help, I've listed topics from various fields below, the underlying idea or human experience that instructors ought to focus on, as well as an example of how students can learn this actively:

Content/Topic (discipline)	Underlying Idea of Experience	Example of Active Learning
Slope (mathematics)	Steepness	Installing a wheelchair ramp (or other steep lines); designing ski slopes that prevent skiing too fast.
Theory of Multiple Intelligence (psychology/education)	We are all "smart" in some way, but not necessarily in school subjects.	Students find out what they are "smart" in through a self-reported questionnaire.
Just-In-Time (operations management)	Efficiency (providing information, services or products as needed)	Have students prioritize their class workload—which do they do first?
Tiananmen Square Protest of 1989 (East Asian studies)	Injustice	Posing a scenario to students where the university sweeps injustices like alcohol-induced violence under the rug.

Immune System (biology, medicine)	Defense	Making comparisons or using metaphors with sports, chess, military, or any activity that requires one to fortify or play defense.
Framing Theory (communication, journalism)	We all perceive something in our own way.	Brainstorm different ways to frame an argument.

See how posing a scenario about university indifference to campus violence can help students relate to protests in Tiananmen Square? While both circumstances are quite different, the underlying idea (or experience) is the same—injustice.

Now go and create your own underlying ideas and active learning examples, using three concepts you plan to teach.

Once you've established the universal ideas or experiences behind the content, organizing the details—the activities you use, the lesson structure—will be much easier. We will discuss this in the next two chapters.

CHAPTER 6

"Touch" the Audience

There is a basic marketing principle that it takes seven "touches" to turn a potential customer into a buyer. The more contact, or "touches," you can have in as many ways as possible, the more likely you will build a strong relationship and in turn sell your product or service. One way might be through repeated advertising; another way might be through sponsorship events; while a third might be through word of mouth or social media. Multiple entry points help consumers internalize the marketing message.

The same goes for learning. Students need various ways to make sense of information. Textbooks alone won't do it. Lectures may help. But the best kinds of "touches" are the most personal and interactive. An effective pharmaceutical rep, according to surgeon/author Atul Gawande, can persuade stubborn doctors to adopt a new drug by "touching" them seven times. He would stock the doctor's closet with free drugs in person:

Then he could poke his head around the corner and ask, "So how did your daughter Debbie's soccer game go?" Eventually, this can become "Have you seen this study on our new drug? How about giving it a try?"[75]

The point is to engage—something we discussed in Chapter 3, *Adopt an Active Approach*.

The instructor's primary role, therefore, is to design meaningful experiences. Whether one adopts an *I, We, You* approach (*I* teach, *We* practice, *You* try it on your own) or a *You, Y'all, We* approach (*You* engage with a problem first, *Y'all* then work together, *We* discuss at the end), experiences crystallize the concept/topic learned. In this chapter, we examine nine ways to "touch" your students:

- Discussion
- Debate
- Small group work
- Surveys/inventories
- Role-play/perspective-taking
- Demonstration
- Student (individual or group) presentation
- Case studies
- Guest speakers

Following are Pro Tips for each of these activities. My purpose is not to address the *what*, but rather, to supply insights on the *how*. As you read them, think about whether they may work for your particular courses.

Discussion: Use open-ended discussion questions (those that have no set answers) interspersed throughout your lecture, rather than all at the end. This cultivates an ongoing two-way conversation between instructor and students. Avoid asking questions with one-word answers—often the "yes" or "no" questions (e.g., "Is Marxism relevant in today's world?") or those that start with *who, where,* and *when.* They stymie participation. Instead, use *what, how,* and *why* questions. (Chapter 9 offers specific ways to optimize classroom discussions, since they are the most used and poorly executed form of activity. As such, I've kept this section on discussions short.)

Debate: These are most suited for controversial topics like race, evolution, and string theory. However, you do not have to follow the traditional debate format (one-on-one, with each person refuting the other). I've had much success dividing the class into two sides and informally asking questions that each side—rather than person—has to answer and/or refute. This puts less pressure on individuals and increases collaboration.

However, some critics believe debates can reinforce existing biases of a subject, rather than broaden students' understanding.

It has to be done right.

One solution is to assign students to argue for viewpoints different from their own. This requires finding out their initial perspectives (perhaps by allowing them to sort into two sides of the room). Those who defend their initial viewpoint rarely consider others' perspectives or change their views.[76] On the other hand, students who were initially neutral or opposed the view they defended were more likely to change their views in support of the side they debated. I remember one student, in a debate on whether kindergarteners learn better through *play* or *pre-academic instruction*, told me that, although she still believed children learn best through unstructured play, she appreciated why some academic instruction is needed, especially among disadvantaged student populations. Isn't that the point of such activities—to broaden perspectives?

I prefer dialogue that emphasizes openness rather than competition, something a *Socratic Seminar* cultivates (see Chapter 9 for details). At the same time, there are a variety of debate formats that can address the criticisms about reinforcing biases,[77] one of which I strongly recommend: the *four-corners debate*.

The *four-corners debate* helps students see the gray areas of a topic. Essentially, students contemplate their opinions of a topic or statement, then move to one of the four corners of a room, which are marked *Strongly agree*, *Agree*, *Disagree*, and *Strongly disagree*. Those who have selected the same corner work together to present arguments for their position. After defending their position, students may decide to switch corners if their opinions have changed. Finally, each group writes a paragraph summarizing the strongest arguments for their position.

Want to know more about conducting a *four-corners debate*? See a K–12 lesson plan—which can easily be modified for higher education—at educationworld.com called "Four Corner Debate."

Other practical ideas (such as the *fishbowl debate*, the *think-pair-share debate*, and the *problem-solving debate*) are presented in an article called "In-Class Debates: Fertile Ground for Active Learning and the Cultivation of Critical Thinking and Oral Communication Skills," from the *International Journal of Teaching and Learning in Higher Education*.

Small group work: This strategy is loosely defined and can include any number of formats. For instance, students can separate into groups to collaboratively answer an open-ended question, work out a problem/scenario, or brainstorm solutions. Four to five students per group tend to balance well the needs for diversity, productivity, active participation, and cohesion. Hold students accountable by having them document their responses. When appropriate, I give each group *chart paper*, which they can use to jot down group ideas and present to the rest of the class. Using chart paper enhances accountability more than using regular paper to jot notes. The nature of the former tends to require more effort than the latter.

I use small group work as my go-to activity, especially when there is limited time to plan. Honestly, it's easier to implement ("What do you think about XYZ? Get into groups of four and discuss") compared with other activities, and it involves the whole class. You get a bigger bang for the buck.

Another type of cooperative learning technique imported from the K–12 world is the jigsaw approach, which takes more time to plan but is infinitely more rewarding. Each individual within the group is responsible for researching or understanding one piece of a topic and then coming together to teach his or her group members. In effect, each person becomes an expert in his or her particular area. In learning about the Civil War, for example, one individual could study the events that led to the war, another could research Abraham Lincoln's Gettysburg Address, while a third could examine the Battle of Antietam. Members have a stake in their peers' work, since they are all responsible for knowing the topic as a whole, not just their individual expertise.

I've found *jigsaws* particularly useful in college-level discussions to broaden students' perspectives. Some call this *perspective-taking*. For instance, how do you get students to see several sides of police–minority conflicts in the U.S. that have dominated news cycles recently? One perspective can be explored from that of minorities, one from the law enforcement community, a third from the broader population, and a fourth from a local councilmember. Students could either research this topic as part of a larger project on community relations, or just as effectively, they could each spend ten minutes imagining what it's like to be a Black man, a police officer, a white person, and a councilmember. In the end, the professor can filter their ideas through the overarching question, *How can we build better relations in minority neighborhoods?*

Have students choose one of the perspectives by counting off ("1, 2, 3, 4 ... OK, all the 1s will take Perspective A; all the 2s Perspective B ..."). Other random criteria like the order of birthdates and names will work too. The point is to force students to take perspectives they are not necessarily aligned to, which in turn broadens minds.

Perspective-taking can be immensely rewarding. Not only does it promote positive interdependence and individual accountability,[78] but through the jigsaw approach it also reflects the way people solve problems in the real world. Each individual brings expertise to a group, just as production, design, manufacturing, and marketing teams collaborate to bring the best possible product to market. Furthermore, the jigsaw method also reflects the idea that the best way to learn is to teach.[79] Peer teaching is an idea of which professors do not nearly take enough advantage.

There are some key considerations to a successful jigsaw classroom.[80] One is to create heterogeneous groups (usually four to six students), diverse in terms of race, ethnicity, ability, and gender. This promotes a better, more tolerant environment that builds interdependence. Another consideration is to appoint a group leader—typically someone who can handle the responsibilities of getting members back together, time management, potential conflicts, and the like. The instructor should provide guidance when necessary, while carefully deferring to group leaders whenever possible. Finally, professors ought to create "expert" groups that consist of other students who have researched the same topic. By comparing notes and discussing, students can enhance their understanding in expert groups. This is particularly useful when a student has trouble doing his or her part.

Watch how two professors apply the jigsaw method to a classroom topic on modern art in "The Jigsaw Classroom Exercise" (5:14) on YouTube.

Regardless of the kind of small group activity, managing groups is critical. Novice instructors typically overlook how much time students need to talk, how to group students, and what each member ought to do. I might say, "OK, get into groups of three. Spend four and a half minutes discussing this question." Note the use of odd and specific time increments. It subtly reinforces the idea that time is valuable.

Unless you have a valid reason, don't make the mistake of letting students form their own groups. Friends will always sit with friends, stronger students will select like-minds, and the weaker ones flounder.[81] Pre-forming groups saves time. I physically walk over and motion to students, "OK, you three make one group, you three make another …"

An alternative is to not mention the need for groups until *after* you've given directions. For example, you might say, "I want you to think about the scenario [I just described] and write down three possible solutions. Get into groups of five based on the following …" You would then separate them based on some preplanned method—by proximity, by number, etc. This minimizes them being distracted by looking around to see who to group with until the last minute—*after* directions have already been given. K–12 teachers know that young learners get easily distracted once the word "group" is mentioned.

Make sure to post written directions as well (on the board, in slides, or as a handout) to facilitate understanding.

Often, I force students out of their seats. Otherwise, the law of inertia—an object at rest tends to stay at rest—kicks in. This is as true for adults as it is for children. Students get a chance to move around, stretch out, and work in new settings and with new people. Fight the natural urge to let students remain where they are, which leads to sluggishness and "status quo" mentality. Ask students to move chairs into groups or an inverted U-shape, for instance. Even during peer teaching, my students would ask their classmates to move around—whether to vote with their feet, stand in a circle, or pair with classmates from the other side of the room. My education students consistently point to this simple adjustment as a valuable teaching tip.

For a highly practical (and FREE) PDF article on making groups, read *Turning Student Groups into Effective Teams* on ncsu.edu. It includes useful forms on team policies, team expectation agreements, and team member evaluations, among others.

What should instructors do during group work?

Move around!

Circulate from group to group to listen in on their conversations. It may feel safe or normal to stay at the front of the room, but "breaking the plane"—the imaginary line that separates the front from the first line of student desks—is critical. It adds energy to teaching. Moving around the room also shows the teacher is actively participating, not just putting groups together so they can take a break. Finally, it enhances classroom management.[82] You want students to know you own the room, so to speak. It keeps students (particularly those sitting in the back) on their toes.

Offer guidance when necessary, but do not interfere, as it can undermine the process of "sense making." You can always provide your perspective later. Listening also allows you to pick up themes to refer to later.

Surveys/Inventories: I was teaching Howard Gardner's theory of multiple intelligences, the idea that people can be "smart" in areas other than academics (e.g., people-smart, body-smart, and visual-smart). Wondering how I could engage students more, I decided, why not have them find out their own strengths? People love taking quizzes about themselves. So I had them take a multiple intelligences survey.[83] I am not talking about formal instruments used in research studies, which can be long, tedious, and inappropriate. We're talking about the kind of polls they already do on Facebook ("What kind of friend are you?"). Learning about oneself through surveys can help students see the topic more usefully.

Search online for existing surveys related to your topic. I downloaded, for instance, a short eight-question "grit" scale in our discussion on perseverance and other non-cognitive skills that contribute to academic success.[84] Students loved finding out how resilient they were. The key is to have them reflect on the results and discuss implications.

Surveys about mindsets, personality, attitudes about writing, and technology use are but a fraction of those that exist online. Check Pinterest for inspiration!

Can't find a survey online that fits your needs? Then create one yourself. Use Google Docs to help you customize surveys and tabulate the results. Start here:

www.google.com/forms/about/

Role-play: During a peer teaching session, one of my students, Katia (not her real name), was teaching her classmates about *transgenderism* (where individuals identify with a gender different from their assigned sex). She asked her classmates to play certain pre-scripted (and at times un-scripted) roles to better understand what transgender children go through. For example, a male student might be given the role of a six-year old boy (Sandy) who identifies as a girl. Another student would play the frustrated parent:

Mother: "Sandy, I ironed your navy pants for school today. They're on your bed.

Sandy: "Mom, I told you so many times, I want to wear a dress!"

Mother: "Sandy, we've been through this already. You can wear a dress on the weekends, but not at school. What would your friends think?"

Sandy: "I don't care what they think! I hate wearing pants!"

Mother (in a resigned voice):   "I'll make you a deal. We will buy you a pink pair of pants ..."

Here, Katia asked audience members to evaluate the parent's approach to the child. The point is that her classmates start to identify transgender struggles as similar to the ones they have with their parents about clothing choice, food, toys, etc. Katia has found an initial way to tap into the underlying human experience behind transgenderism through role-play, which can lead into deeper conversations about the issue. Evaluating a scenario invites students to be active learners.

Role-play can be used to explore one's values (as with the transgender example), to solve a problem (e.g., public policy students playing stakeholder roles in deciding how to address a city's growing crime problem), or even apply skills (e.g., teaching a skill to children, evaluating a patient's medical history, interviewing clients in social work).[85]

Like the jigsaw approach, role-playing can help students with *perspective-taking*. Each participant plays a stakeholder who argues a particular position. For example, if students are discussing politico-social issues like affirmative action in higher education, they could consider the perspectives of a minority student, a majority student who is denied admissions, parents, and the admissions officer. Imagine the different roles that can be used for a variety of social, political, cultural, historical, scientific, or philosophical issues.

The most important part of role-playing is the *post-activity debriefing*.[86] As in any reflection, here is where learning is clarified, confirmed, and solidified. The class reflects and discusses as a group, ideally with the actors getting first crack at discussing their own feelings and behaviors in the role-play. This also gives them a chance to defend against potential or imagined criticisms and protect their ego. Observers can then provide their thoughts.

For a step-by-step lesson plan on role-play, see educationworld.com's Role Play Debate.[87]

Demonstration: Witnessing a phenomenon, whether it is a "human sound wave" to simulate sonar[88] or Newton's cradle to demonstrate momentum,[89] can make an abstract concept concrete—and relatable. What's the best way to make demonstrations instructive? As I often do in this book, I refer to the experiences of K–12 teachers. When demonstrating a math word problem or a scientific phenomenon, we ask students to go through the following three steps:

1. Predict
2. Experience
3. Reflect

When students predict what will happen, they have a vested interest or a stake in the outcome. More importantly, the act of predicting activates their prior knowledge and pushes them to think logically and critically. Students may also discover inconsistencies or weaknesses in their own thinking. The experience (the demonstration) allows students to work out the problem, watch, or listen to what happens. Finally, students reflect, sharing possible explanations and making sense of the experience.

Demonstrations remind me of the grade school "read-alouds." Teachers display a picture book to the class, and children predict the story based on the title and the cover illustration. When finished reading aloud, teachers ask students to re-examine their predictions: Why were some predictions correct and others not?

Interactive demonstrations with math were particularly engaging.

Here's one involving *estimating* I used with third graders during Halloween:

Introduction/Motivation: "Class, take a look at this big jar of candy."

[Students excitedly talk amongst themselves.]

"That's *a lot* of candy, right? Take thirty seconds to study it. What questions come to mind?"

[Inevitably, someone will want to know how many pieces of candy are in the jar.]

Predict: "Good question. Let's count them! But first, let's try to *predict* how many pieces there are. Remember, as you're thinking, ask yourself, *What strategy can I use to 'guess-timate' the total?* Are you predicting based on how many rows you see? Are you grouping them in your head? Are you using multiplication? When you have a number in your head, write it down in your notebook and then explain what you did to a partner."

Experience: "Now, let's count them out." [Teacher pours out the content and counts aloud or has students count along.]

Reflect: "Wow! So we have 128 pieces of candy in the jar. How close did you come? Let's discuss."

Do you see how the process of *predicting*, *experiencing*, and *reflecting* can help students think more critically? Again, I specifically relay K–12 experiences in this book because these topics offer a simplified version of what you will do. It doesn't take much to modify them for a college classroom. And they are equally as appropriate. In many ways, this tri-partite structure—i.e., predict, experience, and reflect—mirrors the way mathematicians, researchers, and other problem solvers work in real life.

The *predict-experience-reflect* structure is an approach I consistently use throughout my course, and demonstrations are a perfect opportunity to do that. Even videos can apply this structure ("What do you think is going to happen in this clip?"). Never blindly go into a demonstration without students predicting and reflecting. Students learn little from passive observations.[90]

Make this part of your routine, whether in demonstrations or another activity. How can you illustrate the concepts in your course as a demonstration?

Student presentations: Simply put, I don't recommend using oral student presentations, even as they are mainstays in college classrooms. Professors often reason that presentations are a great way to learn through "teaching." I agree in theory, but not in practice. The problem is that students do not know how to teach, and as a result, they waste their classmates' time. When they present, their goal is to *demonstrate content mastery*. This means impressing the professor, not their peers. The result is a bored and frustrated class. Students learn very little, I've found, unless they are taught to present or teach constructively. They prefer to hear *you* lecture, not necessarily their peers. If professors find it challenging to keep a class engaged, how much harder is it for students?

With that being said, I do in fact teach my education students how to present, since presenting is closely related to teaching. Peer teaching and presentations are a critical part of my courses. Even then, however, students need consistent practice to engage the class effectively. When taught correctly, student presentations can help both the presenter and his or her peers learn.

See Appendix A and B for two lesson plans on teaching students "how to present."

<u>Case Studies</u>: With the 21st century way we work, no other type of class activity helps students solve real-world problems more than case studies. They organize and bring to life abstract concepts by forcing students to make difficult decisions about complex human dilemmas.[91] Moreover, this problem-based learning approach puts students in the shoes of stakeholders in the same way as role-play (and even the jigsaw) activities.

Case studies are not just for business, law, and medicine anymore. They can be quite creative for all fields. Sociology professor John Foran, for example, uses text from Thucydides' classical epic, *The History of the Peloponnesian War*, to set up a scenario on the first day of class:

The leaders of Melos faced a terrible choice: have their countrymen die as free men or live as slaves. The powerful Athenian generals and their fleet of thirty-eight ships carrying heavy infantry and archers waited at the shores of Melos ready for action as the Melians deliberated.[92]

Students were asked to play the role of the Melian representatives and given ten minutes to discuss their reply to the Athenian ultimatum. Would students agree to submit and become part of the Athenian empire as a colony to protect their people? Or would they insist on fighting against crushing odds for their belief that independence is the greater ideal? What a way to introduce students to sociology!

Identifying solutions to a specific problem makes case studies (or case methods) interactive. Students are putting themselves in the shoes of the character. This particular example of the Melian dilemma demonstrates that case studies can be customized to many disciplines.

How can you use case studies/methods in your particular course?

1. Decide the kind of case you plan to use. If short (like Foran's case of the Melian dilemma), it can be read in class. If longer, consider assigning the case to read as homework with guiding questions (e.g., *Who are involved? What are some of the potential obstacles?*). This will provide ample time to prepare and think. How do you want to divide the groups? Smaller groups (less than five students) allow more opportunity for participation. How long will students deliberate? Make sure to explicitly tell

them how long they have, and follow through. As a student, I hated it when professors didn't tell us how much time we had to discuss with partners. The mindset of a brainstorm with a specified time limit is very different from one that is open-ended.

2. Determine what students are producing. How are students displaying their results? Through presentation or individual papers? Is there a designated individual speaking for each group? Will they need to document their thinking on chart paper, the board, or on notepaper? (Again, writing on chart paper tends to engage groups more.) Make the outcome explicit to help students approach the discussion with more focus and urgency.

3. Provide guidelines on how to approach the case. Should students approach the case as impartial consultants or as one of the stakeholders? Perhaps taking on several roles? Are there constraints on their thinking (e.g., providing solutions based on a libertarian perspective)? Once the approach is established, students need concrete steps (e.g., *First determine the main characters or parties involved. Second, identify the main problem or obstacle. Third, identify the constraints. Fourth, answer the following questions* ... etc.)s Finally, establish or discuss ground rules and specifications (e.g., allowing students to use the Internet as a source; disregarding information not already presented in the case). Don't just let students talk it out. Without structure, they will veer off topic.

4. Facilitate the process. Walk around from group to group, posing questions that get students to work out their thinking ("Have you considered …?"; "Why did you …?"; "What evidence do you have to support …?"). Resist the urge to inject your opinions and expertise. Make a mental note of themes that may need to be addressed later. Apart from guiding, you also need to monitor—break the plane. Are certain students allowing others to take over? One way is to designate roles—with one person as the recorder, one to play the devil's advocate (I highly recommend having one), one to manage the process, time, etc.

5. Synthesize. Bring students together to discuss and/or present their responses. More importantly is to situate their work within broader perspectives or across various disciplines. Using the Melian dilemma case study, for example, an instructor might bring up the ethical responsibilities that come with power. Do students ever have power over others? Imagine the discussion about bullying, hazing, and other relevant student-related issues.

As for finding case studies to use, there is no shortage of websites. Here are some of the more useful ones (including those that have collections), listed by major discipline:

Business
Harvard Business Review (case studies can be purchased for under USD $10—but well worth it): https://hbr.org/store/case-

studies

Knowledgent Perspectives (data and analytics):
https://blog.knowledgent.com/category/case-study/
MIT Libraries: https://libraries.mit.edu/news/business-studies/14576/

Social Science

Social Science Research Network:
http://papers.ssrn.com/sol3/DisplayAbstractSearch.cfm (type in "case study" in quotes in the author, title, abstract keywords search box)

Science

National Center for Case Study Teaching in Science (supported by the National Science Foundation and the Department of Education): http://sciencecases.lib.buffalo.edu/cs/collection/

All Disciplines

MERLOT: Multimedia Educational Resource for Learning and Online Teaching (use the search term "case studies"):
https://www.merlot.org/merlot/index.htm

For more about how to teach using case studies—including liberal arts areas—read *Teaching and the Case Method* (see resources at the end of the book).

Guest Speakers. As a fifth grade teacher, I invited a Holocaust survivor to speak to my students, who had visited a local Jewish heritage museum. Hearing how she managed to escape as a young girl while witnessing her siblings and parents killed left my kids weeping. While this experience may sound traumatizing, it made an otherwise abstract part of history more concrete to children. Years later one of my students, then in high school, said she still remembers that experience.

That's the potential power of guest speakers. Whether survivors of a terrible tragedy or experts in the industry, guest speakers carry a certain credibility that academics often can't match.[93]

To do it right, however, requires two considerations: 1) arranging for the speaker to come; and 2) co-planning the actual talk.

Without proper planning, guest speakers and their presentations can waste students' time. Experts may be unfamiliar with the level of students' content mastery, whether by talking over their heads or being inappropriately introductory. Miscommunication may happen when guests aren't fully aware of the learning objectives.

Below is a cold-call email template to secure a guest speaker. Note it can be adjusted for your use, particularly if you already have some sort of relationship.

Dear ___,

Allow me to introduce myself. My name is Norman Eng, an adjunct assistant professor at the School of Education, XYZ University. I teach a seminar course for fifteen student teachers. At this point in their studies, my students are looking for guidance on their future teaching career. Your authority in this field, as the principal at ABC School, will help them as they prepare a teaching portfolio. My colleague, Dr. Firstname Lastname, recommended I contact you.

I would like to invite you to speak to my students on Thursday, March 24, 2016, from 5:00 to 6:00 p.m. Your expertise will help them focus on the right way to prepare a cover letter, what to include in their teacher portfolio, and what experiences and skills separate good candidates from great ones.

The School of Education will be happy to cover costs associated with your travel [if necessary, you can add *"in the form of a $__ stipend"*].

I would be honored if you would accept this invitation to speak at my class. If you do, I will provide more details, including class objectives and expectations. Please let me know at your convenience if you will be able to join. You can contact me via this email or by phone at (123) 456–7890, if you have any questions.

Sincerely,

Norman Eng
Adjunct Assistant Professor
School of Education

Once a speaker accepts your invitation, contact them via phone, email, Skype, or in person to discuss the specifics. Discuss key points, using the following questions as a guide:

What is the course and/or class about? Send a syllabus or reading to the speaker, so they are aware of what the course is about or what students are expected to know.

What is the class culture? Is it formal or informal? Will students readily participate? Do they know each other fairly well or not? How do you, as the instructor, tend to interact with guest speakers? (I, for one, like to "jump in" when I have something to add, so I mention this to them.) Speakers appreciate knowing the class dynamics and level of collegiality.

What is the objective of this lesson or class, based on the syllabus? How does the guest's appearance fit into what students are learning?

What are the expectations for this lecture? Establish the length of time and the format (thirty-minute lecture plus a Q&A, or more informal interaction with students?). This shouldn't be more than one hour.

What project is the guest speaker working on now that might be relevant and that might help students gain insight?

If appropriate, would it be possible to take photos or film the presentation and make the recording available to both speaker and students? Recordings can be used for the guest speaker's own promotional purposes.

Next, prepare students for the talk. Let them know how this session will benefit them: *Will the speaker give tips about getting a job? What is the industry like? What is a typical day like in the field?* For instance, if my guest is an author speaking at an undergraduate creative writing course, she may describe her daily writing routine and how she overcomes writer's block. Framing the talk in terms of benefits motivates students.

Just as important: ask students to prepare two or three questions. If the class is relatively small (less than thirty students), students can come to the class with questions in hand. In larger classrooms, however, I recommend students submit questions at least three weeks before the event (they can do this on the course website). You can then select and submit to the guest speaker the best questions. Not only can he or she incorporate responses into the talk, the speaker will work harder to customize the lecture.

During the actual talk, students can take notes. Associate Professor Randy Laist at Goodwin College suggests having students compile a list of the three most interesting things the guest said.[94] This allows you to discuss these points afterwards.

Pro Tip: Not ready to invite a big-time speaker? One easy way is to ask the research librarian at your institution to come in. He or she can discuss effective literature search strategies and appropriate citation formats to help your students write better term papers. I learned a lot from my guest speaker the first time I invited our research librarian, even with my years doing research for my doctoral dissertation.

Finally, don't forget to send a thank-you note to the speaker. Better yet, have the class draft one. You'll be sure he or she will come back! Make sure to cc your department chair and/or the head of your program.

Wrap-Up

As you plan activities over the term, consider variety. I typically use discussion as my base activity, for instance, but have used every single activity in this chapter. Which one(s) work with your particular lesson? The more you try, the better handle you will get on choosing the appropriate activities.

With the activity in mind, we can move forward with an outline. Chapter 7, *Craft Your Outline*, will help you write the beginning, middle, and end for two kinds of lessons—a *lecture-driven* lesson and an *activity-driven* one. Stay tuned.

CHAPTER 7

Crafting Your Lecture Outline:
Opening, Middle, End

We devoted the last chapter to detailing ways to engage students, based on your specific topic and essential question. With that, we can start putting together a lecture, lesson, or presentation.

Much of how you craft your lesson outline will depend on whether you use a *lecture driven interactive* approach (similar to the *I, We, You* method in K–12) or an *activity-driven interactive* approach (like the *You, Y'all, We*). Although the latter engages students more actively, the former has its uses. Lectures can be interactive as well, albeit in different ways. Let's look at how to craft your outline—beginning, middle, and end—for each lesson type. Use the blank worksheet templates for both in Appendix C and D at the end of this book.

Lecture-Driven Interactive Lesson

Opening. Student attention is at its highest at the beginning of a lesson. Experts generally suggest presenters and instructors have no more than five to ten minutes at the beginning to connect with the audience,[95] with some saying no more than a minute and a half.[96] Think of the way we read the first few paragraphs of a book or an online article to gauge interest. Poor presenters fail to think through this part. Instead, they put the emphasis on the middle—the "meat" of the presentation. But by that time, audiences have stopped caring.

There are unlimited ways to open a lesson, but I've found six that consistently and immediately engage students:

1. Provocative question
2. Striking statistic or fact
3. Anecdote
4. Quotation or aphorism
5. Analogy
6. Scenario/problem

Here's how I might use each one to start my lesson on Paulo Freire's banking concept—an idea we discussed in Chapter 5, *Develop Your Topic*. (As a reminder, Freire believed this approach to education—where teachers deposit knowledge into students like a bank—robs students of authentic learning.)

Provocative opening question: "What makes a lecture boring to you?"

This question doesn't even bring up the topic of Paulo Freire. Instead, it explores the underlying experience students can relate to—boredom (Chapter 5 details how to make topics more relevant by searching for the underlying idea or experience).

<u>Striking statistic or fact</u>: "People retain only 20 to 30 percent of what they hear. What do you think?"

By introducing an alarming consequence of lecturing, an instructor can set the stage for an intriguing lesson for the banking approach to education.

<u>An anecdote</u>: "When I was taking an accounting course as a sophomore, I fell asleep in class. A lot. As in every single class. And I tried not to. I was a good student. I knew that it left a bad impression. But I couldn't help it. Every class was a boring lecture about debits and accounts receivable. I remembered almost none of the terminology. Does this sound familiar?"*

Stories are one of the most powerful ways to connect with students. Every time I plan a lesson, I think, *Can I insert a story here?* Use them regularly to illustrate your points. For more on

---

* Looking back, I wondered why the instructor didn't ask students to examine a balance sheet as accountants for a client to learn accounting terms. I know it would have been hard, but likely worth it. It reminds me of the psychology professor who asked students to assess her mental health as a hands-on way to learn (see Minaker, 2013).

the power of stories and anecdotes, see Chapter 8, *Create Slides: PowerPoint Strategies.*

<u>A quote or aphorism</u> (written on the board):

Tell me and I forget.
Teach me and I remember.
Engage me and I learn.

What better way to intrigue students than through a quote that can be deconstructed?

<u>An analogy</u>: "You know how we deposit checks? We go to the bank and deposit it into our account. When we need money to pay for a meal, we go to the ATM to withdraw. Education is like banking, according to Paulo Freire. Teachers 'deposit' knowledge like you deposit a check. And then when students need that knowledge, as they might for a test, they withdraw that knowledge just as they would withdraw funds. What do you think?"

Analogies are ideal for illustrating or simplifying complex concepts. When choosing an example, first figure out the general principle you're trying to explain (in the above case, a one-way transfer of information). Then find something, an action or behavior, that illustrates the principle from real life (e.g., a person depositing money).

<u>A scenario</u>: "Let's say your eight-year-old nephew is having

trouble understanding fractions. He is having a test on it at the end of the week. How would you teach it to him?"

Scenarios put students into the shoes of the character and push them to make sense of the situation. That struggle allows them experience first-hand, whatever concept you are teaching.

The first five strategies (question, statistic, anecdote, quote, and analogy) are easy to implement. Scenarios are more difficult to use, since this upends the traditional lecture format. It opens with an activity and then follows with talk (the *You, Y'all, We* approach from Chapter 3, *Adopt an Active Approach*), which makes lessons highly engaging. Regardless, opening your lesson with any of these strategies gets students' attention right off the bat and starts your lesson on the right foot—much better than jumping into an abstract lecture. The last thing students want is for their instructors to start by saying, "So today, we're going to discuss the reading…"

Start jotting down ideas for your opening using one of the six openers—or mix them up. Questions and anecdotes are the easiest to customize to students' interests and implement last-minute. But I encourage you to explore each one, however. Depending on your topic, ask yourself, *Which of these opening strategies would be most appropriate to engage students?*

This will determine how the rest of the lesson flows. Will it be discussion-oriented or some other activity? Typically, instructors incorporate the opening into their PowerPoint lecture (see Chapter 10 on how to use PowerPoint more effectively).

<u>Middle</u>. Much of what we discussed in the last chapter, *Touch the Audience*, goes into the middle of the lesson. What activity or activities are you using—small group work, role-play, demonstrations, surveys, or something else? Which is appropriate? When possible, you can use more than one. For example, after a fifteen-minute lecture on the topic of nature versus nurture, I might have students work in small groups to brainstorm their responses for a debate that immediately follows on how much they believe the environment and heredity shapes us. Another example is having students answer a survey and then discuss their findings among those who had similar responses. As a reminder, below is a list of some activities discussed in Chapter 6:

- Discussion
- Debate/competition
- Small group work
- Surveys/inventories
- Role-play/perspective-taking
- Demonstration
- Oral presentations
- Case studies
- Guest speakers

<u>End</u>. Inexperienced presenters often overlook the ending, yet it reinforces what the audience learns.

There are two ways to end a lecture-driven lesson. First, it can be used to *share* students' work or thinking, which broadens their perspectives. It is as simple as saying, "Let's talk about some of the ideas you came up with." After sharing, remind students the point of the activity by tying everything back to your original opening and how it benefits the student. For instance, you might say, "Remember the question I raised in the beginning of the class about boring lectures? Next time you hear one, think about how you would've engaged students more actively." Or, "From now on, you will never think of teaching or lecturing the same way. You know it's so much more than conveying knowledge; it's more about engaging students and creating meaningful experiences." The ending should connect to the beginning. If it is hard connecting the ending to the beginning, then you have planned too many things to teach (see Chapter 5, *Develop Your Topic*, to narrow your topic).

Second, instructors can use the end of the lesson to *assess* learning. Whether you give students a mini-quiz, or better yet, an "exit ticket" (see Chapter 10, *Fixing Lingering Issues*), you hold students accountable for what they learned. Furthermore, assessments let you know how well you taught. If, for instance, students can't articulate the major factors leading to the rise of Hitler by the end of your history lesson, then chances are, you have either shoehorned too much into that lesson or your lesson did not engage students enough. In my child development course, I end all my lessons with the course question, *How can we help students develop into successful adults?* This ending connects each lesson to the overarching course question and helps students see the point of the weekly readings. Each lesson helps them refine their understanding of how children develop.

Use the *Lecture-Driven Interactive Lesson Worksheet* located in Appendix C to plan your lecture-driven interactive lesson.

Activity-Driven Interactive Lesson

Here, the lesson is essentially flipped from the lecture-driven interactive lesson, by opening with the activity, rather than the lecture. This is the *You, Y'all, We* approach, which engages students right off the bat. This can be used in almost any type of discipline, whether it is creative writing, music theory, archeology, business, STEM, or even language. Your creativity is key. See Appendix D for the template.

Beginning. To open, the instructor presents some sort of issue students can immediately grapple with, whether it is a musical composition, a reading passage, a scenario, or case study. Are you asking students to define a problem, analyze it, or solve it? Such dilemmas can be open-ended (having more than one solution/response) or closed (having only one answer as part of a multiple choice). Either is fine. (See also Chapter 6, *Touch the Audience*, for details on the case study as a way to open a lesson.)

Whatever the activity, students work (or think) *individually* first—the "you" in the *You, Y'all, We* paradigm. They contribute their *own* ideas without influence from peers. It helps those who are introverted or shy in particular. Group work can also frustrate those who process information slowly. These students need time away from extroverted classmates who "spitfire" ideas. To build student accountability, ideas should always be documented on paper.

In terms of time, instructors can give students anywhere from two to fifteen minutes to think/work individually, depending on the purpose and the scenario given.

Pro Tip: Have you ever had students ask questions to answers you've already given? Frustrating, to say the least. To prevent this, get students in the habit of consulting their peers first. Only then may they ask you. In the K–12 world, teachers call this the "ask three, then me" rule. This goes for details on missed assignments as well. Sanity protected.

Middle. After a short period of time, students work in small groups (two to five people, depending on class size)—the "y'all" in the *You, Y'all, We* approach. Here, they can experiment, share their work, and/or collaborate to figure out solutions. Your job, as always, is to facilitate—listening to each group, guiding their thinking with focusing questions, recording examples you may wish to bring up later, and briefly answering their questions (remember to break the plane!).

Once, my undergraduates were brainstorming ways to appropriately praise learners. One student told me, "My parents never praised me. They were strict, typical Chinese parents. But I turned out pretty good. Why does everyone think we need to praise kids? Isn't doing too much of that just as bad?"

I asked her, "What does your group think?" I found out that several of her classmates agreed and decided to bring it up as a relevant topic to this particular class. The point is not to give your perspective too quickly, but allow students to make sense of it with their group and the class.

It is important to also manage the process: How much time do students have? What are the parameters? Have you planned what materials they need (chart paper, Post-it notes, markers, etc.)? Although students can choose partners, I generally prefer to move students around and have them work with different partners, if only to broaden exposure to different peers (see Chapter 6 on how to manage groups). If necessary, ask students to designate who will take notes (either on paper or on chart paper to share later) and who will speak/present. I find that formalizing the process, as opposed to keeping things informal, can help students who need more guidance.

End. The last part of the lesson is the "we" part of the *You, Y'all, We*. Each group gets a chance to talk to the rest of the class and reflect. Your job here is mainly to listen, ask questions, and redirect, not summarize or give your perspective quite yet. You don't want to color students' thinking midway, or before some groups have had a chance to present. Your perspective may lead to cognitive dissonance for one group if their perspective differs.

Afterward, you as the instructor may clarify, summarize, evaluate, and tie students' perspectives to the course content. You may decide to bring up relevant figures and academic terms. And because students grappled with the underlying ideas in the beginning, they will have the background knowledge and experience (i.e., the schema) to appreciate these terms.

It is possible to even have your (short) lecture or presentation at this point—no more than 10 minutes! Here, the instructor goes over the technical details of the issues or concepts that students worked on earlier. He or she might reinforce students' understanding with the vocabulary, industry terms, and expert perspectives from the textbook or from the instructors' experience and knowledge.

For instance, let's say a lecturer is doing a lesson on social class. If she followed an active learning approach, students might talk about their perceptions and experiences of the wealthy, the middle class, and the working class. They might find ways to categorize jobs like a salesperson, paralegal, and electrician into different classes as part of the "hands-on" activity. Only at the end does the professor formalize terms like "the underclass" and "socioeconomic status." She might even show a table of the different categories of social class (e.g., What kinds of jobs are considered middle class? What income level constitutes poverty?). The best professors know that such technical knowledge is not relatable or memorable until students can situate the topic within their world. By organizing the lecture for the end, students can better relate to the material. Imagine flipping the classroom this way for your lessons. Have you ever tried to have the PowerPoint at the end? Try it.

Like many instructors, I did the opposite. My lectures started with PowerPoint. It included educational terms like *perennialism*, *comprehensive high schools*, and *land grants*, or perspectives like the *hereditarian view of intelligence*. Students, I had believed, needed to know these terms if they wanted to be good educators. Yet they never remembered much—no matter how charismatic I was or how entertaining my lectures were (I put a lot of work into making my slides memorable!). In researching about teaching and learning, it finally dawned on me: we don't lecture to young children when we want them to learn something new! We just let them play. They learn to love things like baseball, cooking, ice-skating, swimming, and chess—by just *doing* them. They gain confidence and proficiency through trial and error. Only when children show sustained interest do we then teach the particulars—e.g., the *backstroke* in swimming, the *queen's gambit* in chess, the *double play* in baseball, and *parboiling* in cooking. The terms, the vocabulary, come at the end. Before then, they are meaningless. That's when I realized that lectures serve a better purpose at the end—even for adults. It clarifies and solidifies the activity (or experiences) from the beginning of the lesson.

Alternatively, you may wish to evaluate students' understanding at the end by having them write. If so, provide an open-ended question related to the essential question from the beginning of the class (read about the "exit ticket" in Chapter 10, *Fix Lingering Issues*).

Use the *Activity-Driven Interactive Lesson Worksheet* located in Appendix D to plan your activity-driven interactive lesson.

Timing

How much time should you spend on the lecture versus the activity?

It depends on the type of course and the length of the class. There are no hard-and-fast rules, but one rule of thumb is to spend double the amount of time on activities as on lecturing, leaving aside some time at the end to share, reflect, assess, and reinforce the lesson objective. You should also build in time for miscellaneous elements, such as announcements, breaks, and transitions. Here are some suggestions for segmenting the lecture-driven interactive lesson, based on the length of a class.

If your class is...	Spend no more than this much time on lecture	Spend up to this much time on activities	Sharing/ Reflecting	Misc. Time
1 hour (60 min.)	15 min.	30 min.	10 min.	5 min.
1.5 hours (90 min.)	20 min.	40 min.	20 min.	10 min.
2 hr. 15 min. (135 min.)	35 min. (break up into two parts)	60 min.	25 min.	15 min.

Notice the percentage breakdown: about 25 percent of the time is on lecture and 50 percent of the time on activity. For lengthier classes (over two hours), you may be tempted to lecture longer—i.e., over half an hour. Resist that temptation. People's attention peaks around twenty minutes then steadily decline. It is better to break up a 40-minute lecture, for instance, into two separate twenty-minute chunks.

If engaged in hands-on activities (e.g., group work, debates, and brainstorming), students will appreciate the *lecture* → *activity* → *lecture* → *activity* change of pace. In my one-hour forty- minute math methods course, I break down the class as such (excluding miscellaneous):

Discussion of fieldwork	10 minutes
Peer lessons (students teach and critique each other)	15 minutes
Lecture	20 minutes
Hands-on activity	40 minutes
Reflection	10 minutes

With *activity-driven interactive lessons*, the time allotted for each part is similar:

If your class is …	They should spend this much time grappling with an issue, dilemma, or scenario	Then spend up to this much time working cooperatively with peers	Sharing, Reflecting, and Lecture (if nec.)	Misc. Time
1 hour (60 min.)	10 min.	15 min.	15 min.	5 min.
1.5 hours (90 min.)	15 min.	25 min.	20 min.	10 min.
2 hr. 15 min. (135 min.)	30 min.	40 min.	35 min.	15 min.

Note that these suggestions assume students are working on one issue, dilemma, or scenario in one class. If there is more than one, then you can adjust your timing accordingly. I recommend breaking up class time—especially if it is over an hour and a half—into a few different activities. If you are teaching more than one concept, then you can break up the lecture and activities into small segments.

For example, let's say a sociology professor is teaching about the complex relationship between *social class* and *race* for an introductory course, covered in Chapter 18 of the students' textbook. This professor decides that two major areas best illustrate this dynamic: 1) the school achievement gap; and 2) residential segregation. While there are many other important areas covered in the chapter, the instructor has to "niche down" the topic so students can spend more time exploring and internalizing.

He or she might spend the first ten minutes describing the *achievement gap* in detail (i.e., lecture #1), including how poor minorities tend to have lower achievement. To delve deeper, students will then work in groups to recall their own academic/social experiences with various ethnic/racial groups in high school (i.e., doing an activity). Only after students have shared their perspectives will the professor move onto the second, related topic on *residential segregation* (i.e., lecture #2).

(By the way, who is to say the professor ought to lecture first? S/he could have easily started with a warm-up activity, where students are asked to compare their own childhood neighborhood to a nearby neighborhood that was racially and socioeconomically different. The ensuing lecture on *residential segregation* then becomes an organic outgrowth of this activity.)

Here is how I break down my one-hour forty-minute math methodology course into multiple sections of lectures and topics (assuming class starts at noon):

12:00	Housekeeping/Announcements (5 min.)
12:05	Class reflections (e.g., discuss students' fieldwork observations) (15 min.)
12:20	Activity (e.g., peer instruction) (15 min.)
12:35	Lecture/Discussion (20 min.)
12:55	Activity (35 min.)
01:30	Summary/Share/Reflection/Wrap-up (10 min.)
01:40	Class ends

Segmenting longer classes into smaller, diverse portions keeps students alert. For even longer classes, say those that are two and a half hours in the late afternoon, I might break it up this way:

05:00	Housekeeping/Announcements (10 min.)
05:10	Class discussion/Reflections (20 min.)
05:30	Lecture (20 min.)
05:50	Activity (40 min.)
06:30	Break (5 min.)
06:35	Lecture (15 min.)
06:50	Activity (30 min.)
07:20	Summary/Share/Reflection/Wrap-up (10 min.)

07:30   Class ends

Again, note these are for lessons that adopt a more traditional, teacher lecture style, which should still incorporate as much student activity as possible. I would not recommend the following (using a one-hour class that meets three times a week):

10:00   Housekeeping/Announcements (5 min.)

10:05   Lecture / Discussion (45 min.)

10:50   Wrap up (10 min.)

11:00   Class ends

Unfortunately, far too many instructors informally follow this format. Even if discussions and questions are interspersed throughout, the teacher is still very much dominant. In an *I, We, You* format, the teacher may start the lesson, but he or she shifts the focus to the students. By the latter half of the class, students are actively learning, through some activity.

Action Step

For this lesson, your action step is to develop your outline. Start by considering if your lesson is lecture-driven or activity-driven. Then, define your opening, develop a middle, and finish strongly—using the templates in Appendix C and D at the end of this book. The next chapter will focus on executing and optimizing your slides, discussions, and other activities.

PART 3

Execute and Optimize

CHAPTER 8

Create Slides: PowerPoint Strategies

Welcome to Part 3 on lecturing and engaging your students more effectively. Before we move forward, let's take a quick review of how we got here.

Part 1 focused on laying the groundwork—the idea you are teaching *students*, not *content*. As such, you are thinking from their perspective: why are they taking your course? What do they hope to gain? What are the obstacles? Answering these questions can orient you to a *student-centered mindset*, a progressive (if not overused) term in the K–12 world. We contrasted this with some of the common problems in lectures and presentations in the collegiate world that often turn students off.

In the third chapter, we talked about a better way—one based on *active learning* where students grapple with a situation or problem (a *You, Y'all, We* approach) rather than listen to the instructor present first (similar to the traditional *I, We, You* method of instruction).

One way students learn actively is to tap into the universal ideas and experiences that underlie the content. So instead of teaching about *discrimination*, why not recall students' prior experiences with discrimination as the lead-in? Another way is to have students investigate solutions to problems. So they might devise solutions for someone with *levoscoliosis* (curvature of the spine to the left), for instance, rather than merely memorize its symptoms.

Part 2 helped to develop your lecture/lesson in detail: How to *niche your topic down* to the most important parts to create the *guiding question*. It needs to also align with the course benefit and students' Big Picture Goal. We also discussed the structure of your lecture and outlined an opening, middle, and end.

Now we head into the third section, which is about executing and optimizing our lecture and presentation. This chapter will deal specifically with slides (particularly PowerPoint). I won't go into other slide alternatives like *Prezi* (prezi.com) or *PechaKucha* (pechakucha.org), since they have not yet entered mainstream use. If you use either, email me your thoughts.

Remember some of the problems of lectures/slides that we referred to in Chapter 1—that they are too long, too dense, not relatable, and reading directly from slides creates boredom? We'll go over strategies to overcome these challenges, starting with *Show, Don't Tell.*

Show, Don't Tell.

Audiences rarely remember what presenters say. One common strategy to address this, according to presentation experts, is to "say what you are going to say, say it, then say what you just said."[97] This means you preview what your presentation is about (the roadmap that manages your audience's expectations), then you present your material (the lecture/presentation), and then finally you remind them what the main points were (conclusion). A simple 1-2-3 template that focuses on repetition. But this is only the beginning.

When K–12 teachers teach young children to "show, don't tell" in their writing, children learn to make their writing come alive. Why tell readers, "Carla was angry when she heard the referee's whistle," when you can "show" them?

My face turned white. My heart sank. I knew right there and then, my shot came too late.

See how the second sentence *shows* Carla's anger without explicitly *telling* it? Describing emotions enriches the imagination. Presentations are no different: rather than elaborate on the content students are supposed to know, *show* them. Talking about global warming? Instead of layering facts onto one slide, why not show a video clip of plunging ice shelves in Antarctica or an illustration of U.S. coastal lines in 2050?

But you may ask, *Don't students need more content?* Not necessarily. That is what the readings are for. Your presentation is not a rehash of the textbook, but an entreaty for deeper engagement—to get students to reflect, to question, to wonder. Whereas the readings give students the content, the lectures/presentations make *sense* of the content. Chapter 10, *Fix Lingering Issues*, will go over ways to ensure students do the readings.

Take a look at this slide:

This is What A Typically Snooze-Inducing Slide Looks Like

- The first bullet point is a full sentence.
  - The sub-bullet point backs up the main point.
  - So does the second sub-bullet point.
  - And the third.
- The second bullet point is another new point.
  - Which is backed up with another full sentence.
- There's at least a third bullet point...
- ...If not a fourth. Usually, they are full sentences.
- Often times, there are no pictures. Just text.
- No one reads any of these sentences.

If your slides look like this, an overhaul is needed. Let's start with some basic rules:[98]

1. Less is more—always use short phrases or word(s) in your bullets, never sentences (think of bullets as newspaper headlines: impactful, attention-getting, and concise).

2. You, as the speaker, provide the specifics.

3. Avoid sub-bullets. (Do you need bullets at all?)

4. Leave plenty of empty space (makes it easier for the audience to absorb text).

5. Do you even need words? Would a picture or video work better?

The idea behind these rules is that people generally avoid reading text, especially if it is dense. The addition of visuals makes it easier to absorb.[99] In content-heavy situations like classrooms, your job is to simplify and make sense of content while engaging deeper thought, not to "reinforce" what they have already read. The higher expectations—the accountability in learning—should take place in your discussions and your activity. Your communication, therefore, should always be focused and concise.

Often, good presentation is about *how* you show your content, rather than *what* you show. Look at this slide:

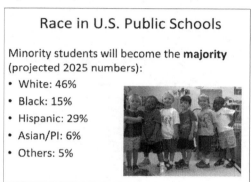

Race in U.S. Public Schools

Minority students will become the **majority** (projected 2025 numbers):
- White: 46%
- Black: 15%
- Hispanic: 29%
- Asian/PI: 6%
- Others: 5%

Not bad—at least the photo's relevant and the text isn't too heavy. But why not make the statistics more visual, less work for students to grasp? Like a table:

Race in U.S. Public Schools

Minority students will become the **majority**:

White	46%
Black	15%
Hispanic	29%
Asian/PI	6%
Others	5%

Much easier on the eyes. Notice I took out the reference to the year 2025—why not just say it? Saying exactly what is on the slide makes it harder for audiences to remember.[100] Remember, slides are not a dumping ground for your notes.

The next slide is even better.

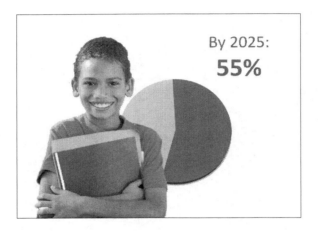

It shows more than it tells. Details like the percentage breakdown by race can be omitted—you can say all of that out loud. The less clutter, the more audiences can focus on your point. This is what experts call the *coherence principle.*[101] Simpler slides may require more planning, but they leave a deeper impression. Isn't that reason enough?

Pro Tip: Are your slide images public domain or creative-commons-licensed? If not, the copyright owner can ask you to remove the photo or sue you (however unlikely). Most images found on Google search are *not* public domain or openly licensed for reuse. See the Creative Commons education website on how to do searches properly on Google, Flickr, Fotopedia, and other image sites.[102] (See the resources page at the end of this book for other websites to search images) Other free public domain images can be picked up from the Library of Congress.

What do you think of the following slide?

Herbert Spencer
(1820-1903)

- Spencer's ideas about education influenced by Darwin's *Theory of Evolution*: Survival of the fittest.
- Wanted schools to compete against each other.
- Believed people in an industrialized society needed a utilitarian education.
- Introduced rationale for curriculum development based on promoting health, social relationships, and economic productivity.

This is a fairly typical slide. But there's still too much to read. Students will copy every bullet point ("Wait, wait! Go back!") and barely listen to the professor. How can you improve it? One way is to make it inherently interactive. Below is one option:

The law is the survival of the fittest . . . The law is not survival of the 'better' or the 'stronger,'. . . It is the survival of those which are constitutionally fittest to thrive under the conditions in which they are placed; and very often that which, humanly speaking, is inferiority, causes the survival.

- **Herbert Spencer**

You might think, *That's a lot of text as well.* But here, students will actively deconstruct Spencer's quote on "survival of the fittest"—and then discuss it. They will likely learn more about Spencer than through bullet point slides.

Finally, think of using videos as another way to *show, don't tell.* Effective professors use them as launching points or supports. Some students may struggle with reading, so hook them with the non-written word. Diana Laufenberg, executive director of the non-profit Inquiry Schools, recalled a student in her high school class who knew how to think critically but, because of learning issues, struggled to read and write. As a result, Laufenberg introduced her lessons with a visual—including interesting or puzzling videos, sometimes even short ninety-second videos to grab students' attention. It got them to wonder and gave them a little more background so that even if they were doing the assigned reading, students came to the topic with their own questions.[103] Chances are, you have a couple of students with similar learning issues every semester.

What does a *show, don't tell* presentation look like? Watch Steve Jobs's introduction of the iPhone (51:18) at the MacWorld Conference in 2007, particularly the first ten minutes. How does he get an audience so worked up? How much text does he (not) use? How does he employ visuals? Think about how you can apply his techniques to your lecture.

Fixing the Common Problems

Remember the common problems with lectures we discussed in Chapter 1? They're too long, they're too dense, presenters use slides as teleprompters, and they don't connect with the audience. When lectures are created as slide presentations, these problems can really disengage students. Let's look at some solutions for each one.

It's Too Long. We all make this mistake. And when students present, it's just as bad. In fact, length is such an issue that two entrepreneurs created a new presentation approach called PechaKucha where presenters can't exceed twenty slides and each slide appears for no more than twenty seconds. *That* forces presenters to be concise.*

So plan how long your presentation will last. A useful rule of thumb is the *10-20-30 Rule*, popularized by presentation expert Guy Kawasaki: Use no more than ten slides in total, have presentations no more than twenty minutes long, and use type size no less than 30-point. It's a handy guide—and I emphasize *guide*—that you may decide to deviate from. But if you stick to its underlying message—keeping slides short and sweet (and large enough to see)—then your students will appreciate it.

Some experts even recommend telling your students in the beginning how long your presentation will last to manage their expectations. It's up to you, as long as it doesn't interrupt your opening gambit or your lesson flow. If you have to go less than 30-point type size, then it's an indication to split the slide into two, or

---

* I don't necessarily recommend PechaKucha for classroom lectures, because it prevents in-depth interaction. Yet, more research needs to uncover its benefits in the classroom. I'd be curious to hear other instructors' experiences with this presentation software (http://www.pechakucha.org).

that you need to cut something out. How often do instructors try to squeeze information into one slide—which makes it hard for students to read? They won't bother. Large type also prevents the next problem—slides that are too dense.

Use the 10-20-30 Rule: No more than 10 slides. No more than 20 minutes to present. No less than 30-point type size.

It's Too Dense. Avoid more than one point per slide, supported by no more than three bullet points (if necessary). With visuals and graphics, you may not even need bullet points. Seth Godin, the author of *Really Bad PowerPoint*, goes so far as to argue that no slide should ever have more than six words. If you need to have several bullet points, why not space them over a few slides instead of jamming them into one? Another alternative is to make bullet points appear one at a time (through "Animations," found under "Slide Show" at the top or in the ribbon toolbar). You don't want your class jumping ahead and reading every bullet while you are still discussing the first one.

Have you ever heard absent students say, "Don't worry. I'll just read your lecture from the PowerPoint"? If so, your presentation has failed to do its job. Presentations aren't supposed to be a standalone document that flows from beginning to end. Otherwise, why do students need you? Your slides should support what you say, not the other way around. That's why students can't miss your class—

because what you say enriches their understanding of a topic. They can't get that from the reading. Why bog down your presentation with details students could have gotten from the reading or the textbook?

If you insist on a "leave-behind" or something students can refer to, give them a separate paragraph handout summarizing your topic, or a brief—and I mean *brief*—outline that they can add notes to.

 Pro Tip: Go through one of your existing presentations slide by slide. If readers or the audience can discern your whole lecture from your slides, then you, the instructor, are superfluous! You might as well just give them the slides and go home. Time to rework them.

Not Relevant. Chapter 5, *Develop Your Topic*, is devoted to making topics relevant, so I will not belabor the point. Instead, I will ask you to consider incorporating more stories in your presentation. Unlike dry facts, stories make people care. Veteran radio personality Ira Glass perhaps best summed up the power of anecdotes:

No matter how boring the material is, if it is in story form … there is suspense in it, it feels like something's going to happen. The reason why is because literally it's a sequence of events … you can feel through its form [that it's] inherently like being on a train that has a destination … and that you're going to find something …[104]

Glass believes a good anecdote should 1) raise questions and 2) provide a moment of reflection. Questions are the bait that implies a forthcoming answer—one that keeps the audience wanting more. Second, audiences need to be able to see the payoff. When they do, there is a "light bulb" moment that connects with them and leaves them more enlightened than they were a moment ago.

When lecturing on the topic of verbalizing to children, I share with students an overheard conversation on the bus between a father and his young son, who was no more than five. In vivid detail, the boy described how a girl in his class was bullying him. She picked on him in lunch and pushed him around in the playground. Yet the dad never sought to advise. He kept probing and questioning, as Socrates might do with his pupils. "What do you want to do about it?" the dad asked. The young child cocked his head, raised his index finger, and responded, "First things first ..."

I mean, what five-year-old says that?

My students laugh at this boy's precocity even before I finish what he says, which doesn't even matter at this point. More important is that the anecdote leads to a productive discussion of how verbally rich environments affect children's development as active sense-makers and problem solvers. This child was clearly surrounded by people who encouraged verbalization. Students see this better in story form.

Interestingly, you can even present a research study as a story. Sticking with this topic of verbalization, I retell the following:

In the 1990s, two researchers, Betty Hart and Todd Risley,

went into the homes of over forty families to record what parents say to their babies. Some of the parents were doctors and lawyers, some were from the working class, and others were very poor. Hart and Risley wanted to see if families with higher socioeconomic status interacted differently than those in the lower SES. So they recorded interactions during playtime, during meals, and even while parents were doing chores. After recording and codifying all the data—thousands of hours' worth—they found surprising differences between the classes.

By this point, students are engrossed. Questions have been raised in their minds about the differences in interactions among classes, as well as how they themselves were raised as kids. Students have a chance to reflect and predict the results from the study (summary: parents in the upper/professional class spoke 2,153 words per hour, more than three times the words spoken by parents in welfare—only 616—which cumulatively lead to a thirty-million word gap by the age of three[105]).

The statistics don't matter so much as the connection to the topic students feel. It propels them to learn more. Uniting an idea with an emotion through storytelling is the best way to make a topic relevant.[106]

Reading Directly from Slides. Finally, the last problem is presenters who treat slides as teleprompters. Don't use it as a dumping ground for your notes.

If you use notes, PowerPoint's *Presenter View* can help. There you can jot notes at the bottom. When you summon Presenter View, you can see your current slide, your notes for that slide, the running time, and even preview the next slide. The audience only sees the current slide.

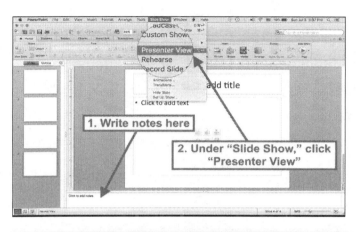

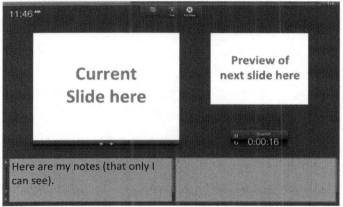

When you are starting out, or teaching a new course, Presenter View can be especially helpful. The more you practice, however, the less you'll need it. Furthermore, having notes can sometimes constrict interaction; it is as if I'm reading from a script. This undermines my ability to stay in the present, to stay flexible, and to adapt to cues.

To end this chapter, I'll leave you with a little homework. First, go watch the TED Talk playlist on "How to tell a story," which breaks down some of the components of good storytelling. Second, read the article "What Makes a Presentation Great? Deconstructing an Awe-Inspiring TED Talk" by Meghan Keaney Anderson, which deconstructs great presentations. I recommend you take a look at both when you get a chance.

CHAPTER 9

Optimizing Discussions

The world in language is half someone else's. It becomes "one's own" only when the speaker populates it with his own intention, his own accent, when he appropriates the word, adapting it to his own semantic and expressive intention (M. M. Bakhtin, literary critic and semiotician[107]).

I once overheard a student ask a classmate, "So what did you do in science yesterday?"

"Nothing," responded her classmate. "We just spent the whole class talking."*

---

* I overhear a lot of insights when I come to my own class early—something I advocate instructors do whenever possible. Students just forget you are there as they're waiting for class to start. You hear their frustrations, their obstacles, their assignments, almost always related to their other classes. Far too many professors

Students don't always see the value of class discussions. Learning, they believe, only happens when the professor lectures. You need to change that perception. *Discussions are not a waste of time*, I tell students at the beginning of each term. Speech is an expression of thinking, and only when students use their own words to describe a concept do they truly internalize it (as Bakhtin's quote above suggests). Ultimately, getting students to talk is not just to check for understanding, but also to develop thinking.[108] The more they talk, the deeper they think. The best teachers, therefore, spend more time listening.[109] Truthfully, I still struggle to do this.

The problem comes when there's no structure—when you simply allow free talk. Certain students dominate, others go off on tangents, and then soon enough no one remembers the original question. You start getting opinions and arguments, rather than facts and reasoning. That lack of structure is why students think discussions are a waste of time. Here are seven methods to bring structure, accountability, and depth:

1. Post the discussion question(s) visibly.
2. Request students come to class with a written question, quote, or comment from the reading.
3. Arrange seats in a circle or semi-circle.

---

wait in their office until five minutes before class starts. They are missing a prime opportunity to learn more about their audience, which can shape their instructional approach.

4. Vary questions along Bloom's Taxonomy.
5. Challenge students' responses.
6. Teach students that not all opinions are equal.
7. Use Socratic seminars.

Post the discussion question(s) visibly.

Seeing questions on the board (or in your slides) reminds you, as well as the class, to stay on topic. Students quickly forget questions posed out loud. When they go off tangent, *point* to the question and say one of the following:

- "So, let's get back to this question…"
- "What Jimmy said makes sense, yet it doesn't quite address this question."
- "How can this discussion help us answer the question on the board?"

Request students come to class with a written question, quote, or comment from the reading.

I call this the QQC (question, quotation, or comment). This could be a *question* students want to delve into, a *quotation* that resonated with them, or a *comment* or *reaction* they had to a specific section. Not only does this ensure students do the reading, it focuses the discussion on their terms. Moreover, this strategy minimizes the chance they come unprepared. Pair the QQC with the *cold-calling* strategy to ensure diverse perspectives (see Chapter 10, *Help Students*

Succeed). I encourage students to add questions or comments that pop up to their list throughout the discussion. This encourages learning as a continuous, rather than a one-time, process.

Arrange seats in a semi-circle or circle where possible.

An open, face-to-face forum prevents "hiding" and facilitates accountability. For the instructor, the key is to vary where you sit throughout the semester. If you sit at one spot every time, those in your line of vision feel constantly under pressure to participate. Students on either side of you, meanwhile, get little attention. The consequence? They feel less safe opening up.

Vary questions along Bloom's Taxonomy.

Asking students to remember facts from the reading (e.g., "What is meant by *sunk cost*?") is not enough. Use questions that help them understand, apply, analyze, and evaluate. Such types of questions are based on Lorin Anderson and David Krathwohl's revision of Benjamin Bloom's classic 1956 taxonomy of cognitive skills.[110] Here are examples of prompts that can be used in questions:

Bloom's Taxonomy of Questions	Prompts
Knowing/remembering	Who is? What is? Where is? When is? List, define, tell, label (tends to have closed or limited responses)
Understanding	Describe, identify, explain, discuss, retell

Applying	Demonstrate, interpret, dramatize, illustrate, relate, translate How would you? What would you [do]? What would happen?
Analyzing	Why?, compare, contrast, classify, investigate, what evidence can you find?, etc.
Evaluating/Creating	What do you think?, criticize, judge, can you assess?, based on what you know …

Challenge students' responses.

Simply asking, "Why do you say that?," "What makes you think that?," or even "What do you mean?" pushes students to elaborate, clarify, and think more critically. The very process of articulating will crystallize their understanding. Don't settle for the first thing they say, even when it sounds obvious. I sometimes play devil's advocate (or pretend to be ignorant), particularly to those with strong viewpoints:

Student: "I think it's obvious there's a balance between the way nature influences us and the way the environment does …"

Instructor: "How so? How do I know if one of them has slightly more influence?"

Redirecting student responses (or questions) allows two things to happen: 1) students will take responsibility for their own learning by talking it out, rather than rely on you as the expert; and 2) additional time for you to catch your breath and think, especially if you need time to respond.

Teach students that not all opinions are equal.

If they were, we would take everything children say seriously. Educator Michael Strong argues that:

> If one accepts all statements as equally valid, there is no reason to be thoughtful or considerate or creative or accurate when one makes statements. There is no reward for thoughtful, well-considered opinions. There is no recognition of the possibility of good judgment.[111]

We teach children to think through their thoughts, consider other factors, and use factual evidence for one reason:

To make good judgments.

Without this ability, we buy the wrong things, select the wrong friends, marry the wrong people, and take the wrong jobs. How many people do we know who always seem to be a bad judge of character?

A thoughtful, well-considered opinion gets more respect. Through the process of discourse, the best opinions (will hopefully) prevail. Isn't that why we have meetings and conferences? No wonder Bloom's Taxonomy considers *evaluation* the highest level of critical thinking. We judge what people say all the time. Students therefore need to be accountable for their opinions.

My theory courses are discussion-heavy, so early on I ask students, "What is the difference between a fact, an opinion, a belief, a preference, an assumption and a bias/prejudice?" Here, students question widely heard expressions like, *Everyone is entitled to their opinion*. They recognize that people tend to confuse preferences ("I prefer using TurboTax") and biases ("Paying taxes sucks") for opinions ("The tax codes need to be reformed"). Classroom discussions, therefore, need to be informed—i.e., based on facts.[*] Here is a breakdown of the six types of assertions, along with examples:

	Definition	Examples
Fact	Can be verified; testable	Air travel is safer than car travel (data back up this assertion).
Opinion	A judgment or conclusion (which may be based on facts yet may need more testing)	It is better to fly to Washington, D.C., than to drive there.

---

[*] Hence the well-known quote by author Harlan Ellison: "We are not entitled to our opinions; we are entitled to our informed opinions." (see http://harlanellison.com/buzz/bws006.htm)

Bias/Prejudice	A narrow opinion based on insufficient or unexamined evidence (but can be tested)	Women are bad drivers. Certain groups commit more crimes.
Preference	A liking for one alternative over another that is not necessarily based on facts	I like driving more than flying.
Belief	Conviction based on cultural/personal faith, morality, or values (cannot be tested; not necessarily based on fact; cannot be disproved; should be minimized in class discussions)	Abortion is murder. There is only one right religion.
Assumption	Universally accepted truths that may or may not be based on facts (can sometimes be based on misinformation)	Large cars are safer. Never swim right after eating.

Because students typically rely on opinions, I tell them to beware the *vividness effect*, the tendency to believe that their experiences (or those of one particularly influential person—such as family, friends, and celebrities) are more valid than empirical data.[112] Research on the safety of airplanes, for instance, can be easily dismissed by one survivor's harrowing experience. So I recommend students support their opinions with textual evidence more than with personal experiences. Otherwise, their statements are beliefs, preferences, biases, or even assumptions. They should be minimized.

Use Socratic seminars.

When my students read the first chapter of E.D. Hirsch's *Cultural Literacy*, they come to class with only a vague sense of what *cultural literacy* means. The same thing happens when they read about Lev Vygotsky's *zone of proximal development*. Students "kinda" know what the concept means, but ... not really.

The Socratic seminar (or Socratic circle) is ideal for unpacking these complex ideas. It asks students—not teachers—to pose questions. Through dialogue, participants collaborate to arrive at a broader understanding. Persuading others is verboten. Better to say, "I wonder if ..." or "Yes, and ..." than to say, "I disagree, because ..."

How are Socratic seminars structured? Typically, there is an inner circle of students and an outer circle (see below). The inner focuses on exploring the meaning of a previously read text through prepared questions and dialogue. The outer circle observes, evaluates, takes notes, and/or acts as coaches to an inner partner. This is similar to the "fishbowl" strategy K–12 teachers use to get outside students to observe and learn from the inner circle students. The instructor guides the discussion where necessary and evaluates the progress.

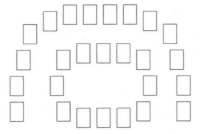

The rules of dialogue are fairly simple: respect the speaker and the group; give peers a chance to speak (especially those who are reluctant); ask new questions only after the previous topic has been exhausted. Only one person should speak at a time. Students may direct questions to the group or even ask individuals specific questions or to clarify ("Millie, what do you think?").

Some helpful Q&As to run Socratic Seminars:

What happens when students don't speak or know what to say? In the beginning, students may find it difficult to run the discussion, particularly if they are accustomed to teacher-directed lectures. Restrain from filling in the silent gaps. Students need time to take ownership of the conversation. Once they see the onus is on *them*, the dialogue will pick up. Furthermore, they will have prepared questions to draw from. If necessary, you may facilitate with questions like, "Alexis, what do you think?" or "It might be helpful to think in terms of …"

What happens if the discussion veers away from the text? This will happen. As long as the students are discussing the *issue* underlying the text, then let them be. For example, students may digress into issues of power when discussing *cultural literacy* (i.e., Who ought to shape our common cultural language?). That's fine. Where necessary, instructors may bring the class back on task.

Is asking questions the only way to structure Socratic seminars? No. In fact, I encourage students to prepare a mix of questions, comments, or quotations from the text. Sometimes an intriguing passage or a reaction may jumpstart a conversation, as this student demonstrates:

> "I really liked when Rousseau wrote, 'Man is born free, and everywhere he is in chains.' I think it means that even though people are born free, social forces like our culture, our customs, our conventions, and our laws make it hard to do what they want to do. But I'm not really sure. What do you all think?"

What about students who feel self-conscious or shy? There will always be students who regularly contribute and others who do not. Encourage reluctant participants to ask the questions (which they have prepared beforehand) instead. This helps them feel they are starting the conversation, and eases them into the dialogue. Often, I end up circling back to the questioner: "Jonah, I'm not sure if your classmates have answered your question. What do *you* think?" This allows him or her a chance to elaborate.

Quieter students may feel more comfortable asking a follow-up question such as, "Can you give an example?" or "Can you elaborate more? I'm not sure I understand." At the very least, this helps to facilitate the conversation. Using names on tent cards can also help personalize the interactions (see Chapter 10, *Help Students Succeed*, for more on tent cards).

Finally, it helps to have quieter participants start the seminar with a question, comment, or quotation. Interestingly, it is easier to talk in the beginning when there is less competition to speak up.

As a last resort, I hand out a preparation guide (with several questions I pose) that students can prepare answers to beforehand—on top of their own questions, comments, and quotes. This guide then structures the dialogue (although in many ways this approach somewhat defeats the purpose of the student-driven seminar). Their written answers make it easier to participate.

See the video "How to Get Started with Socratic Circles #2minPD" for more information (3:40).

Wrap-Up

This chapter explored seven ways to bring structure and accountability to discussions. Which ones do you currently use?

Which ones may enrich your class discourse? Take some time to try them out. For further reading, check out some of the top resources on optimizing discussions, many of which are FREE, at the end of this book.

In the last section, we delve into the day-to-day issues that college instructors face—creating the right learning environment, dealing with students who don't do the reading, enhancing student participation, assessing for learning, giving feedback, and more. Without knowing how to respond to these challenges, instructors cannot help students learn and do well. Don't let these "little things" derail your lesson.

PART 4

Help Students Succeed

CHAPTER 10

Help Students Succeed

Busy (or novice) instructors focus too much on the meat of the course—the content and the delivery. However, subtle factors can slowly unravel student learning and satisfaction, if overlooked. This chapter deals with these issues. Again, I turn to the principles which are familiar to K–12 teachers but often taken for granted in the higher education environment. What can professors do better in the classroom? We discuss five issues:

1. Create a safe and supportive learning environment
2. Get students to read
3. Assess yourself and your students regularly
4. Communicate expectations and feedback
5. Increase student participation

Issue #1: How Do I Create a Safe and Supportive Learning Environment?

If you've ever wondered how to get students to participate more, you cannot gloss over this issue. No strategy or tip will make up for an environment where students feel embarrassed, rejected, or punished for speaking up. It's about building trust.

Maya Angelou once said, "I've learned that people will forget what you said, people will forget what you did, but people will never forget how you made them feel."

Rarely have I heard an expression so true. We all remember how our favorite teachers made us feel, even if we don't remember the details from the course.

When 217 faculty members at the University of Maryland were surveyed about their biggest concerns on the first day of class, three questions popped up most frequently:[113]

Will the students get involved?
Will they like me?
Will the students work as a class?

When students were posed the same question, similar responses were given:

Will I be able to do the work?
Will I like the professor?
Will I get along with classmates?

Interestingly, faculty members incorrectly thought that students were more concerned about whether they would get a good grade, whether the work would be hard, and whether the class would be interesting.

The lesson is clear: *both students and teachers yearn for connection.*

Yet instructors spend little time building this, preferring in many cases to "dive right into the work." Unfortunately, students are still figuring out what kind of course they have walked into and what kind of teacher you are during the first few classes. They're still skeptical. *What happens when I open my mouth? Will someone* (instructor or classmate) *embarrass me? Reject what I have to say? Punish me for speaking up?* Students need to be reassured.

That's why K–12 teachers spend all September building "classroom community"—playing games, doing exercises, having daily rug meetings, etc. They understand that productivity comes after students feel safe around each other.

Google researchers reached the same conclusion when investigating why certain teams in their organization do better than others. The best ones had high "average social sensitivity," the ability to intuit how others feel based on the tone of their voice, their expressions, and other nonverbal cues.[114]

When members feel psychologically safe to bring up new ideas, everyone contributes—not just a few—and the team's collective intelligence improves. Otherwise, people clam up and retreat into their own agendas.

The same applies to a classroom environment. When college

instructors are approachable and understanding,

> They [can] make, or rather give you a sense that you can achieve
> what you are striving for ... if [teachers] aren't approachable the
> students become afraid to ask questions ... This suggests that
> the students' notions of an effective teacher are predicated on
> their seeing themselves as partners in learning, not recipients of
> knowledge.[115]

Think of your classroom climate along a continuum, as seen below.[116] The way you talk or behave sends either a marginalizing or centralizing message. Students perceive *marginalizing* messages by professors as those that exclude or discourage them or their perspective in some way. *Centralizing* messages are more welcoming. *Explicit* comments are direct and intentional whereas *implicit* comments refer to those that were indirect or unintentional.

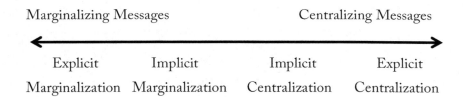

Marginalizing Messages   Centralizing Messages

Explicit	Implicit	Implicit	Explicit
Marginalization	Marginalization	Centralization	Centralization

For instance, students who feel *explicitly marginalized* might have heard racist, sexist, or homophobic comments by professors. On the other hand, female students may feel *implicitly* (or unintentionally) *marginalized* when instructors avoid calling on the women in class. *Explicitly centralizing* messages are those where the instructor purposely brings up (or shows special interest in) different perspectives. Finally, when a professor responds well to perspectives brought up by students, he or she demonstrates *implicit* (indirect) *centralization.*

In their study of LGBT perspectives, researchers Christopher DeSurra and Kimberly Church showed that *implicitly marginalizing climates*—those that unintentionally exclude others—were most common across college classrooms.[117] Is it possible you are indirectly or unintentionally negating students' perspectives? This includes their enthusiasm, curiosity, and participation, which can lead to environments that feel less safe and supportive. Too many times, students just don't feel comfortable sharing. When teachers denigrate, ridicule, or respond sarcastically, students disengage.[118] Where do you fall on this continuum?

A safe and supportive environment engages students. It makes them curious, enthusiastic, and willing to participate. Students will contribute meaningfully in discussions, which enhances the overall classroom learning. One good sign that you've established a safe and supportive environment is when usually quiet students speak up unprompted. This won't happen if teachers fail to manage the class or cultivate a safe environment.

Once, while discussing the impact of testing on student learning, one of my undergraduates said, "I always forget everything after a test. With this class, I actually remember."

Seizing on an intriguing moment, I asked her why.

"Because we just focus on learning. I actually read the article because I know the class is going to be interesting." Others nodded in agreement. This student clearly felt comfortable saying this out loud. More importantly, she was validating a simple truth: learners are intrinsically motivated when the course material is relevant, the teacher is enthusiastic, and they feel psychologically safe.

Instructors therefore should cultivate a safe and supportive environment in every part of their communication—from their syllabus to their demeanor to their instructional approach. Such consistency across all communication—as marketers do when they sync their message in print, broadcast and digital media—makes the message evident. Let's discuss some specific ways to help.

Establish the Right Culture (and Impression) the First Day

One way to do this is to get to know your students—a strategy that improves teacher-student bonds, motivation, and even achievement.[119] Here are some specific ways you can do this.

1. Learn students' names. Even if you have a large class, calling even some names whenever possible will already establish a certain culture—that students are individuals who matter, rather than merely numbers.[120]

 Pro Tip: Some college system rosters online actually display photos of students next to their names. If you have access, print them out and study them or use them as reference. If you haven't checked, talk to your administrators.

The simplest way is to create name *tent cards*.[121] Fold 5×8 index cards in half and write students' names on both sides of each card. Have students put their tent cards on the desks and collect them at the end. Since I arrange students' tables in a U-shape (good for discussion-based classes), the tent cards help students talk to each other and address one other by name.

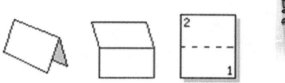 

2. Play icebreaker activities. One activity many K–12 teachers play is the *Name Game.* While a bit cheesy, the Name Game is effective—even at the university level—and most students get into it. It works well for up to thirty students (approximately 45 minutes). Anything larger will take over an hour. The rules (or at least my version of it) are as follows:

1. Start at one end of the room. The first student introduces themselves by their first name along with a word that describes themselves. That word must also start with the same letter as their name. For example, Michelle likes to play Minecraft or Greg likes to watch *Game of Thrones.* (HINT: give students a minute or two to think before starting the activity. You don't want them figuring out a descriptor when they're on the spot.)

2. Each following student has to remember the previous student and description before introducing themselves ("Greg likes

Game of Thrones. My name is Jeanie and I was born in July").

3. Remembering all the names that come before is the challenge. The last student, therefore, has to remember everyone's names and descriptions. To make it fair, I volunteer to go last. After that, I also randomly choose someone from the beginning to recite all the names (HINT: tell them beforehand). This forces the first few students to continue paying attention.

Even when students forget a classmate's name, they often remember the descriptor ("Hmmm ... I remember he likes *Game of Thrones* ... Greg!"). You'd be surprised how this translates into students addressing each other by name during group discussions.

Another icebreaker that builds classroom community is called *This or That*. Education blogger Jennifer Gonzalez describes it as the following:[122]

In this icebreaker, students are prompted to either line up in some particular order (by birthday, for example) or gather in "blobs" based on something they have in common (similar shoes, for example). What's great about this game is that it helps students quickly discover things they have in common. It's also ridiculously easy: Students don't have to come up with anything clever, and they can respond to every question without thinking too hard about it. This game keeps students moving and talking, and it builds a sense of belonging and community in your classroom.

Here are some prompts you can use for This or That:

- Line up in alphabetical order by your first or last names.
- Gather with people who have the same eye color as you.
- Gather with people who get to school in the same way as you (car, bus, walk).
- Line up in order of your birthdays, from January 1 through December 31.
- Line up in order of how many languages you speak.
- Gather into three blobs: those who have *lots* of chores at home, those who have *a few* chores at home, and those who have *no* chores at home.
- Gather with people who have the same favorite season as you.

You can also use surveys or questions that reveal students' interests, which can then inform your lesson plans, communications, and student interactions. PanoramaEd.com has a free online survey that can show instructors and students how much they match. Students love to see what they share in common with classmates.

For other first day activity ideas, particularly for STEM and statistics courses, see:

www.stat.columbia.edu/~gelman/research/published/smiley1 2.pdf

---

3. *Cultivate a growth mindset.* How else can you create a safe and

supportive learning environment? Within the first couple of classes, I emphasize what psychologist Carol Dweck calls a *growth mindset*, the idea that abilities can be developed through effort, good teaching, and persistence.[123] Too many students exhibit a *fixed mindset*, the limiting belief that abilities are innate and cannot change. For instance, how many of us think we are simply bad at math? If so, you are exhibiting a *fixed mindset*. That's a problem. We might be subtly reinforcing a fixed mindset in the way we talk. When students sense this, they stop trying.

Learn more about the growth mindset in the animated video "How to Help Children Fulfill Their Potential" (9:59), which Dr. Carol Dweck narrates. What ways can you cultivate this mindset among your students?

Unfortunately, too many people think this way. At least 40 percent endorse a *fixed mindset* (while another 40 percent believe in a growth mindset).[124] They believe no matter how hard you work or how well you learn, one can never be "good" at basketball, photography, or chemistry, for instance, even though intelligence and talent can in fact be cultivated.[125] Fixed mindset people hide their mistakes or conceal their deficiencies by getting defensive, discouraged, giving up, or fleeing. Have you ever heard students say, "I'm bored"? It's a good bet they're afraid to try, according to Dr. Dweck.[126]

How might you be subtly undermining students' motivation?

Those with growth mindsets, on the other hand, believe that mistakes, challenges, or setbacks are a natural part of learning. Even if one can never reach the heights of scientists like Albert Einstein or athletes like Serena Williams, it does not mean one cannot improve. As such, educating students up front about the growth mindset will improve the class's learning environment. Dr. Dweck provides one way:

> I teach a freshman seminar here at Stanford every year on mindsets. For one assignment I have the students do research on their hero and find out whether the hero was so famous or successful because they were naturally talented or whether they in fact had to overcome a lot of adversity and work really hard. Not once has it ever been the case that their hero coasted.[127]

One easy thing you can do is to change how you respond to students, whether in discussions or in your written feedback. Resist the urge to praise their intelligence (or, for that matter, anything inherited like their looks and their socioeconomic status)—which they may perceive as beyond their control. These compliments tie their worth to things that cannot change and reinforce a fixed mindset. Instead, praise their *effort* and, more importantly, *specific things they did*—elements students can control. Here are some examples.[*]

Instead of saying or writing …	Say/write this …	Explanation
"Wow, you got an A—you must be so smart!" "Brilliant essay." "Great job!" "Excellent!"	"I like how you supported your argument by citing the text."	Students may internalize labels like being smart, which ironically prevents them from attempting harder problems. Also, general platitudes do not enable students to grow. Being specific in what students did well (or not so well) can help them grow.
"Great effort! You tried your best."	"OK. What can you try next?"	While praising effort is better than praising intelligence, it doesn't go far enough. Push students to find other strategies and solutions. Let students know that the point isn't to get it all right away. The point is to grow their understanding step by step.

---

[*] Many of these suggestions have been embraced by the K–12 industry and can be easily modified for higher education.

"I'm sorry, that's incorrect." "Nope." "That's dumb." "That makes no sense."	"It looks like you're getting there …" "You're almost there …" "Not yet, keep going."	When students answer incorrectly, respond in ways that encourage (or expect) them to persist.
"Not everyone is good at math. Just do your best."	"When you learn how to do a new kind of problem, it grows your math brain!"	Reinforce the idea that challenges are an opportunity to grow. For college students, you may want to talk about neural pathways strengthening the more they persist.
"Don't worry, you'll get it if you keep trying."	"That feeling of [math] being hard is the feeling of your brain growing."	If students are using the wrong strategies, their efforts might not work. Plus they may feel particularly inept if their efforts are fruitless.
"Wow, I can't believe you just said that" (in a sarcastic tone— often to a comment that was outlandish or unpopular).	"Why do you say that?" "What do you mean?"	Asking students to clarify (or at least think twice), is better than belittling or passive-aggressively responding.

	"When you persist, you will know more math on Day 30 than you did on Day 1. Imagine how much better you will be in one year."	
"If you work hard in math, you can be like Albert Einstein."		Posing unrealistic goals can have the opposite effect, especially when you compare them to superstars. Instead, push them to compare only with themselves.

Source: Parts adapted from Dweck (2015)

Do you have a *fixed* or *growth* mindset? Even though people likely have a mix of both, this survey will enlighten. See if any of these questions describe how you interact with students: http://mindsetonline.com/testyourmindset/step1.php

The growth mindset phenomenon has overtaken the K–12 industry, with lesson plans and professional development workshops designed specifically to help teachers instill such mindsets in their students. See the link at the end of this book (under Resources) for lesson plans and videos to teach the growth mindset. If one student changes the way he or she thinks, your lesson will be worth it.

4. Other ways to promote a safe and supportive classroom environment: Here are eight more research-based strategies adapted from the book, *How Learning Works: 7 Research-Based Principles for Smart Teaching*:

<u>Make uncertainty safe</u>. Validate different perspectives, discourage black-and-white perspectives, and embrace nuanced thinking. This also means resisting a single right answer. One way is to encourage students to articulate their perspective first before you give yours, so as not to bias them.

<u>Recognize individuals</u>. Students are accustomed to talking to the teacher, not to each other. Encourage them to direct their comments to each other and refer to their classmates by name. Aside from that, take the time to email individuals once in a while and appreciate their work or participation. Be specific:

Rahman, what you said in class today about _____ really made me think about _____.

Jabari, your written reflection really captured _____. Would you mind if I use excerpts as an exemplar for future students? They can learn a lot from _____.

Model the language, behavior and attitudes you want students to embody. Avoid using masculine pronouns for both males and females, explain native idioms to non-native speakers, and include subtitles when showing video clips (I found that useful in classrooms with non-native students). I explicitly call attention to what I do: "Did you see how I asked you all to 'turn and talk' before responding? Effective teachers do this to give their students a chance to verbalize their thoughts."

Another effective strategy is to paraphrase a student's response (and then ask them if you've understood them correctly). Not only does this force you to listen more attentively, it models active listening skills you want your students to have: "So Ritsuko, you're saying that ..." or "Just to make sure I understand, Alexa, you're asserting that ..." This makes other people feel you aren't simply going through the motions of calling on students. Students sense when you are scanning for other participants before they've even finished talking. I'm guilty of doing this. When it happens to me, I feel like a second-rate citizen. Paraphrasing what students say signals to others the importance of listening actively.

Use multiple and diverse examples. Remember how instructors can implicitly marginalize students (see earlier in this chapter)? This means they unintentionally create a negative atmosphere by what they say. When giving examples that involve names, I consciously use the opportunity to reflect a more inclusive environment, with names like Amare, Omar, or Haru, rather than simply using John, Jane, and Jennifer. Plan examples that cut across backgrounds, whether it is gender, culture, or orientation. This helps students connect to the content. It also reinforces their developing sense of competence and purpose. Always ask yourself, *How else can I incorporate multiple and diverse examples?*

Establish and reinforce ground rules for interaction. You want students to feel a sense of fairness and inclusiveness is in place, even when they are running the discussion. Rules can be incorporated into the syllabus and/or generated by students as part of a class discussion (something many K–12 teachers learn). Some sample ground rules:

- Ask for clarification if confused.
- Avoid interrupting others (or raising your hand) when they are speaking.
- Critique ideas, not people (note: one way is to use "I" statements such as "I feel …" rather than "you" statements, which may make others defensive).
- Offer opinions only if you can illustrate with example or support with evidence.
- Avoid put-downs, even if they are done sarcastically or humorously.
- Build on one another's comments and work toward shared understanding.
- Speak from your own experience, rather than generalize.
- If you are offended by anything said during class, acknowledge it immediately.

Do not ask individuals to speak for an entire group. I once asked a Chinese student in my education class about her experiences taking the grueling nine-hour, two-day college entrance exam in China known as the *gao-kao*. "How did students in China feel about it?" I asked her.

"I don't know. I guess they hated it," she responded simply. Later, it dawned on me that she might feel uncomfortable being identified publicly to be the classroom authority on issues assumed relevant and unique to her ethnic group. This also applies to gender, ethnicity, religion, sexual orientation and any other identity label. Those singled out may feel a certain tokenism at play.[128]

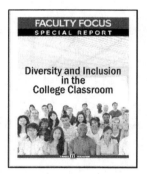

For more ideas about creating *inclusion* (e.g., managing microaggressions, defusing student resistance, and cultivating inclusion in the online classroom), refer to the FREE Faculty Focus Special Report, *Diversity and Inclusion in the College Classroom* (see link in the resources section at the end of this book).

<u>Anticipate and prepare for potentially sensitive issues</u>. Telling students up front that a "hot topic" may have personal significance will manage their expectations. You may wish to explain why this topic is important to the course and remind them of the ground rules to ensure a civil discussion. Neglecting to forewarn them may lead to uncomfortable silences and resentment.

<u>Address tensions early</u>. If you are inadvertently marginalizing, shutting people out, or offending their sensibilities, address the issue before it gets out of hand. This may mean apologizing for yourself or others (for example, "I'm sorry if my comments sounded as if ..."), taking a student aside after class to explain the impact of a comment, explicitly discussing the tension ("Some people believe it is racist to say ..."), or using questions to explore ("What are other ways people might perceive the statement?").

In a discussion about the impact of graduates' grade point average (GPA) on hiring, I once mentioned that grades had little influence on employers' hiring decisions. One student came up to me after class, frustrated because she had worked hard to get back on track after starting out with a low GPA. She didn't want to believe that her effort was in vain. I quickly apologized and clarified that grades were important insofar as they reflected that students cared about their work.

It reminded me to: 1) always remain vigilant in what I say (rather than be flippant) and 2) explain exactly what I meant—that while grades had little to do with one's hire-ability, it did serve as a gatekeeping mechanism in many cases. Demonstrated performance and outcomes were even more important, something I made explicit to this student. Talking to her immediately, however, was critical to alleviating her concern.

Issue #2: How Do I Get Students to Read?

Educator John Warner echoed a problem we all share when he asked, "Is there a more common lament among college instructors than, 'Why won't students just do the reading?' "[129] It doesn't matter if they are high school students, undergraduates, or graduates. Research shows only one-third of students do the readings on any given day.[130] What is happening with the rest?

They aren't necessarily lazy. In fact, students are actually quite rational when it comes to prioritizing their workload. They're thinking: *Will I be tested on the reading? Do I really need the reading for the homework? Will I have to "personally and publicly respond" to the reading in class?* If none of these apply, then they're unlikely to invest their time and energy to read, according to Catherine Small,[131] who wrote *My Freshman Year: What a Professor Learned By Becoming a Student.*

Aside from relevance, students will likely read if the following three criteria are met:

1. They get some sort of satisfaction from the reading (either intrinsic satisfaction—e.g., *Now I know more about a topic I've always had an interest in*—or satisfaction from mastery/accomplishment—e.g., *Now I know how to do this!*);

2. They feel they can understand the material—i.e., it is not too hard; and

3. They perceive their environment to be supportive.[132]

If students enjoy the topic but can't understand the text (which happens a lot, especially in first- year courses and in schools with diverse populations), they won't read. If students understand the text yet it's boring or irrelevant, they won't read. Even if these two conditions are met, students may not be motivated to read or participate if they know teachers judge them harshly.

Don't forget that students have other courses to take—sometimes four or five others. Studying for a test for another class will take priority over your non-graded, discussion-based reading. "Hard deadlines" always take priority over "non-deadlines." Again, students are rationing their time and energy.

So how can you make it easier?

<u>First, think about whether your readings are appropriate</u>. Are the texts truly at the students' level? Are they too hard? When I first taught my child development course, I used the handout on Jean Piaget that some of my colleagues previously used. I hated that text, because it was boring and wordy—for the students and for me. Later, I found a chapter on Piaget from another book that was clearer and easier to understand. Textbooks are often geared to both undergraduate- and graduate-level students in an effort to appeal to more professors, so make sure to review them and ask for your colleagues' perspectives. Remember, just because you have no

problems reading a text doesn't mean your students won't have problems.

Keep in mind the lesson from Chapter 1—*know your target audience*. What kind of readers do you have? What is their level? Plan your texts accordingly.

Second, create a supportive learning environment. Once, I assigned students to read an article called, "Why Americans Stink at Math." One student, in her reflection essay, said she had been previously assigned the same article for another course. The difference, she said, was the excitement in my voice and the curiosity I expressed at hearing students' thoughts. Upon reading this article, she wrote: "I was drawn into every sentence, either agreeing, laughing, or reminiscing about my elementary school memories; the tone clarified to me that the tone, attitude, and amount of passion an educator provides is what affects the abilities and level of comprehension of a student."

Do you simply assign the readings? Or do you preview it? Students won't read if teachers will just end up going over the material next class—as Terry Doyle argued in his book *Helping Students Learn in a Learner-Centered Environment*—or worse, completely gloss over much of the topics they just read. Students need to know that the reading is relevant and that there is a purpose. You might say something like, "Next week's reading is 'Why Americans Stink at Math.' If you think you're just not a math person, this article will surprise you." Of course, not all readings will offer an immediate hook. The point is to connect them to common experiences that intrigue your students.

Third, focus students with guiding questions. Do this ahead of time so students don't go into the reading blind. They have something to scan for or at least keep in mind as they read. You can announce (or write) the focusing question at the end of class for next class's reading or, preferably, write them in your syllabus's weekly assignments calendar.

Focusing questions remind me of the *anticipation guides* K–12 teachers use, which helps students preview the reading. They can be questions or statements that stimulate or activate prior knowledge. I suggest keeping the questions broad—rather than technical (which students will not care about). Something like: "As you read the Piaget handout, ask yourself, what would happen if you …?"

Fourth, ask students to respond to the text in some small way as they read. Ask students to prepare (on an index card or piece of paper) a *question* (what they don't understand, or would like to pose to the class), a *comment* (some sort of reaction to a particular paragraph or agreement/disagreement with the author), or an intriguing *quote* they can share. You may decide to have them do all three or a combination of them. Professors may have students submit these questions on course websites like Blackboard and Canvas. In particular, reading questions show promise in getting students to read.[133]

Also, hold students accountable by asking them to explain *why* they chose their particular question, comment, or quote. To add further accountability, collect them or have them submit them online. Comment on their index cards or grade them as part of their participation score. If you do, hand them back in a timely manner. For some, however, collecting the index cards and responding to them is time consuming.

I prefer to leave five to ten minutes at the end of each class to share these questions, comments, and quotes. Five students are randomly chosen. Depending on how they responded to the text, we may discuss, answer, or comment. If you do this, however, consistency is the name of the game. Every class must have time for sharing. That, along with randomly calling on students (see *Issue #5: How Do I Get Students to Participate [More]*, later in this chapter), ensures that they will read. Without this consistency, this inevitability, students feel less compelled to read.

Will some students just choose a quote without reading the whole article, or give perfunctory comments? Of course. But if the steps from this book are followed, these incidents will be minimized.

Finally, any text responses assigned should be short. Anything long (over a page) diverts the attention from the reading. The writing response becomes a separate, burdensome assignment. You want them to focus on interacting with the text. Feedback from my students over the years suggested too many of them ended up trying to write the same points over and over but in different ways just to fill up the two-page requirement, which wasted their time.

What about quizzing students? I'm fascinated by how students prepare for quizzes. Before class starts, I see them quizzing each other, like such:

"OK, the four stages of Piaget's cognitive development are sensorimotor, pre-operational, concrete operational, and formal operational. Sensorimotor is from birth to age two and describes how children discover relationships between their bodies and the environment. Pre-operational is when ..."

And I shake my head. *They'll literally forget everything after the quiz.* Truthfully, I don't even remember all the specifics of each stage—and I *teach* this! Do my students really get the significance of Piaget's theory? More importantly, do they know how to apply it to the classroom?

I don't use quizzes much anymore—at least not for the purpose of forcing students to read. Short reading responses—asking questions and reflecting—are better to get students to engage with the text more meaningfully (see previous section for details). Quizzes won't do that.[134] Moreover, they reinforce the notion that the only kinds of readings that matter are the ones attached to grades. Quizzes kill morale and goodwill.

That doesn't mean they're useless, however. It depends on how you use quizzes. For instance, in *team-based learning* (TBL), instructors use *readiness quizzes* (or *readiness assurance tests*) at the beginning of class. While they ensure students have read the material, these quizzes aren't being graded. Instead, students work as a group to answer the quiz questions after they have tried it themselves. These quizzes therefore help students collaboratively work out issues that aren't clear and foster deeper understanding.

The key is to determine if quizzes lead to deeper learning. Why do you use quizzes?

Issue #3: Are Your Students Really Learning? (Let's Talk Assessments.)

Years ago, I was immensely proud of my slides. My PowerPoints took hours to develop and incorporated pictures and interactive videos. I used stories to illustrate abstract concepts. I asked probing questions. No question my marketing background played a role. When students participated, I felt my hard work pay off.

None of it mattered, apparently, when my students bombed the multiple-choice midterm. That jolted me. *How was that possible? We spent a whole class learning the differences between pragmatism, realism, and idealism! What happened?*

Students eventually told me there was just too much content to remember—even if the content was engaging. In the end, I found that midterms, like quizzes, did little to benefit students.[*] They served *my* purpose only. Good instruction only goes so far. Even if it improves learning, it won't guarantee it.

What I needed to do was simpler: *check in on students periodically*.

That's the beauty of *ongoing* (or *formative*) *assessments*. They focus

---

[*] I understand that term exams are often necessary or even mandatory, especially in large classes or in courses that require proficiency in technical knowledge (e.g., medicine, law, accounting). All I'm suggesting is that when we don't incorporate content with experience, students will not remember much.

on development, not outcomes. They answer the question: *Are students actually learning?* The answer can guide future instruction. Formative assessments would have told me my education students weren't absorbing all the content, despite the beautiful PowerPoints. My slide lectures set them up to fail. In the end, I was inadvertently failing them.

When you assess your students, do not ask them questions like, "Does anyone have questions?" or "Is that clear?" Students rarely speak up, even if they're unclear. The following are better methods.

1. *Exit tickets* (sometimes referred to as exit slips or minute papers[135]) are a great way to diagnose your instruction and students' learning at the end of each class. There are two ways K–12 teachers approach this:

- Have students answer one to three broad (but quick) questions about what they learned in class that day related to the lesson's "essential question" (e.g., *What is Paulo Freire's concept of banking?*, *Explain Vygotsky's Zone of Proximal Development in one or two sentences*).

- Exit tickets can also help teachers see what students had trouble with. Ask them questions like: *What part of the class was unclear? What questions do you still have about today's lecture?* Students will answer more honestly when writing individual responses.

Poor responses across the board suggest you need to reteach. If only a few students have trouble, ask them to come in during office hours or before/after class. Students' responses can shape your next lecture, by clarifying misconceptions, informing the pacing, or establishing what students learned. When used regularly, exit tickets hold students accountable. In fact, their questions can plan your lesson. Unfortunately, many professors teach the content and then move on. I promise, your students absorbed less than you think.

 Pro Tip: Format exit tickets four to a page using Microsoft Word's two-column formatting (make sure to check the box marked "Line Between"). Questions can be written on the front and in the back. Print out double-sided and cut with scissors. Smaller tickets make it easy to skim through and reduce paper waste. Want a template? See Appendix E.

2. *Entry tickets* are similar, but used in the beginning of class to activate prior knowledge about a topic. More importantly, they focus students' attention to the day's topic ("Based on today's reading, what is your understanding of...?")[136] and inform you of possible misconceptions. Often, students' existing knowledge about a subject hinders their understanding of new concepts.[137] Here is the chance to examine their prior knowledge and clarify.

3. *Creating your own student feedback survey* is a powerful way to assess what worked in your course and what didn't. These are not your official department-wide student evaluations, but ones you customize. It should include both Likert-scale type questions that range from *not useful* to *very useful* (or *strongly agree* to *strongly*

disagree) to open-ended questions. Some instructors use these anonymous surveys in the middle of the semester to gauge or "correct course," while others use surveys at the end of the term to inform their approach the following semester. Both are useful. Allow twenty minutes for students to fill out individually and anonymously while you wait outside the room. Have an envelope where they can submit. If needed, they can drop surveys off to the department administrator to hold onto until the end of semester.

The key is to tailor it to your specific course. I separate the survey into three parts—*instruction*, *assignments*, and *general questions* (See Appendix F for a sample template).

The *instruction* section focuses on pedagogical approaches or techniques, such as lectures, Socratic seminars, student presentations and class discussions. They will vary depending on what you teach (for instance, I use Socratic seminars for theory-based courses, but not for methodology courses). After students rate each one, ask them one or two open-ended questions about which one was the most useful and which one was less useful. This allows me to see patterns in students' thinking about instructional approaches to modify, based on concrete answers.

The *assignments* section finds out whether students think your assignments were helpful (e.g., text responses, final paper, group project, fieldwork reports). Again, I follow these questions with open-ended ones asking which assignments were most and least useful and why. Several semesters ago, for instance, I found that my two-page text response assignments (which at the time were used to make sure students reflected on their reading) were simply not useful and/or too hung up on requirements (such as copying a passage from the text and including at least three different reflections). Students *knew* text responses were a way to ensure reading compliance, and this did not foster learning. From that, I found better ways to get them to read, such as posing questions and reflecting briefly (see the *Get Students to Read* section in this chapter).

Finally, the *general questions* section captures anything you believe might have helped students and want their feedback on. For example, I devoted a workshop session to teaching students "how to present" (see Appendices A and B for sample lesson plans) after discovering that student presentations were poorly planned and executed. Qualitative and quantitative survey feedback suggested I should conduct workshops every term.

One rule of thumb: If at least three students (based on a class of 20–25) say similar things, whether positive or negative, start paying attention. It may represent the class perspective. For example, I've had several students complain that submitting ten fieldwork reports (documenting their public school classroom observations) was overly burdensome and often overlapped. I agreed and cut it down by half. Pay attention to the trends, not necessarily the outliers. Be ruthlessly objective and ask yourself, *Why would students say this?* Have you considered their workload? This, again, goes back to knowing your target audience and the world they live in (see Chapter 2, *Focus on the Student, Not the Content*).

Pro Tip: Leverage any high ratings you receive from these surveys, including the departmental evaluations. I select data to incorporate into cover letters, my LinkedIn page, and other professional sales pieces. One sentence might sound like the following: "Based on written feedback surveys, 94.5 percent of my students over the past three semesters rated my use of lesson studies as 'very useful' to their pedagogical development." Hard numbers bolster your credibility and image.

Sometimes, the course surveys validate an instructional approach or assignment that I'd put a lot of work into. I found, for example, that having students "teach" a topic to their classmates (peer teaching) really helped first-year education students gain practice in teaching, something they rarely encountered until the latter year of the program. This led me to document and present a case study at a national education conference. I wouldn't have known how powerful this approach was without asking students specifically about it. Official student evaluations would not have led me to see this.

Over the long term, these surveys are a powerful tool to validate and refine my teaching approach. If you incorporate one new assessment this semester, use this. It will give you the baseline data, or foundation, for how to approach your course next term.

Equally important is the way you conduct the feedback survey. Let students know up front that this is designed to help them and future students. You want their honest opinion and only want to include elements that will help them learn and gain something from the course. When done, follow up with them. Let them know what you discovered. You don't want them to think that their opinion has been forgotten. They should feel as if they are actively shaping the course in some way. Students chuckled once when I admitted, "Class, I hear you loud and clear ... the textbook was too expensive!"

 Pro Tip: When I go through students' survey responses, I quickly jot down the two or three things I learned and write them *directly on my copy of the course syllabus.* This way, when next semester rolls around, I pull up the syllabus—with my quickly scribbled notes from the student surveys—and know exactly what to modify for the new term.

Get real-time feedback during the class. Have you ever wondered if students are really learning? Even with lively, interactive class discussions, I'm plagued with thoughts that students are only "kinda getting it." They "kinda" get Vygotsky's *zone of proximal development*, they "kinda" know how to use different voices in creative writing; they "kinda" understand the principle of *transmissibility of forces*. Which is another way of saying they don't get it. By the time I read students' final papers, it might be too late.

Enter the *formative assessment.* Here's where you periodically check for understanding throughout the lesson, rather than waiting until the exam, the paper, or the final project (i.e., the summative assessment). Formative assessments may be ungraded and informal.

They let you know where the class stands and allow you to modify instruction on the fly.

Here are various ways to do this:

- Intermittently, ask students to briefly summarize what they had just discussed, whether in writing or out loud ("So, can someone briefly tell us what the *zone of proximal development* is about?"). Professors often assume students "get" the content just because it has been discussed.

- Pair up students to answer one or two questions about the topic just discussed (tip: questions should push them to apply what they learned to a real-life situation). Have them talk to their partner and add to each other's understanding ("Yes, and also …").

- Have students write one question about what is unclear on a slip of paper. This forces them to find weak spots in understanding.

- Use the "Yes, and …" strategy for pairs. Students answer a formative assessment question (e.g., "What is the *zone of proximal development?*") in pairs. When one student responds ("I think it's the area between what children know and what they don't know"), the partner adds on, using the words "Yes, and …" to expand their understanding of the topic ("Yes, and that area is the part that teachers need to scaffold."). Both continue to take turns until there is no more to add on.

 **Pro Tip:** As students participate, periodically ask other students what the participant is saying ("Amir, what do you think of what Sung-Hee said?"). If they missed it, either go back to the participant or ask a third student to clarify. Then, return to the student who wasn't clear or paying attention. Involving several students in one line of response spreads accountability to listen and to understand the topic. Having one student answer correctly doesn't mean others get it. Randomly picking other students to paraphrase, add on, or repeat increases the odds. This is the *cold call* strategy to hold students accountable for participating (see *Increase Student Participation* later in this chapter).

I also provide on-the-spot feedback when students are presenting—usually to praise specific things they did (e.g., starting with an agenda, incorporating videos and images for support, involving classmates, minimizing texts in slides). Depending, I might even say, "I noticed when Frances posed a question, only one or two hands went up. What are some ways she can increase that?" As future educators, my students appreciate having practical on-the-spot feedback, which they can immediately practice. Find ways to give nonjudgmental feedback, and let them know it is in the spirit of helping not just the one person, but the whole class, improve.

Another way is to survey students through interactive technology, such as "personal response systems," or *clickers.** By asking questions and having students respond with their clickers, teachers can view their computer screen as it tallies the clicker responses. They can then decide how to give appropriate feedback to the class.[138] (For more on clickers, see the resources section at the end of this book.)

How do you use clickers? See this video from Dr. Russell James from the University of Georgia: "Using Clickers In the Classroom" (9:46) on YouTube.

 Pro Tip: Those without clickers can use *Google Forms* to create surveys that students can access on their cell phones. Results can be shared in real time just as with a clicker. See the resource link listed at the end of the book.

---

* Clickers are one of the few instructional tools in this book I have not used. As such, I defer to the experts.

A second alternative to clickers is to use color-coded index cards. When asked about their level of understanding of a particular topic, students can raise a green card (*concept is understood*), a yellow card (*concept may need some clarification*), or a red card (*concept requires better explanation*). Simply scanning the room for these colors can indicate where the class stands. This also reinforces the idea that the color-coded system reflects your ability as a teacher to clearly communicate, rather than the student's ability to understand. Students will more honestly respond.

Have students review each other's work. If you've ever graded research papers that were simply not up to expectations, then *peer editing* is a great idea. It enhances the quality of student work before final submission, as well as helps students recognize and address their own weakness when they apply what they see in other papers to their own work. As an added benefit, this assessment tool lightens your workload. The key to its effectiveness, however, is to provide students with clear and specific instructions for what to review— otherwise they are editing blind. I've adapted a sample guide from *How Learning Works* (by Susan Ambrose et al.), which you can modify and hand out during peer editing sessions:

To the reviewer: The purpose of the peer review is to provide targeted feedback to the writer about what is working and what isn't.

1. *First Read: Familiarize yourself with the paper by reading it all the way through without marking it.*
2. *Second Read:*

a. <u>Underline</u> the main argument

b. Put a check mark (✔) on the left column next to pieces of evidence that support the argument.

c. Circle the conclusion.

3. *Third Read: Respond briefly to the following questions:*

   a. Does the first paragraph present the writer's argument and the approach the writer is taking in presenting that argument? If not, which piece is missing, unclear, understated, and so forth?

   b. Does the argument progress clearly from one paragraph to the next (i.e. is it logical and sequential)? Does each paragraph add to the argument (that is, link the evidence to the main purpose of the paper)? If not, where does the structure break down and/or which paragraph is problematic and why?

   c. Does the writer support the argument with evidence? Please indicate where there is a paragraph weak on evidence, evidence not supporting the argument, and so on.

   d. Does the conclusion draw together the strands of the argument? If not, what is missing?

   e. What is the best part of the paper?

   f. Which area(s) needs the most improvement (e.g., the argument, the organization, sentence structure or word choice, evidence)? Be specific so that the writer knows where to focus his or her energy.

I use peer editing in both my advanced seminar classes and

introduction classes, which allows students time to review at least two or three other classmates' work. Attach your peer edit guide sheet along with blank spaces they can fill out and staple to the back of each student's paper. This will increase the odds that students receive balanced and quality feedback. I hold reviewers accountable for their comments by requiring them to sign their initials on every piece of writing they evaluate. Students submit their final paper along with the peer-edited draft/comments.

Pretest students on the first day (or at the beginning of each unit). In my math education course, teaching candidates had to pass a departmental proficiency exam before moving forward in their education program. It was designed to make sure they were competent enough to teach math to elementary school students. So I gave them a pretest assessment on the first day of class. "This will let you know where you stand and what to focus on," I told them. Students appreciated this, especially when the pretest was ungraded. Before they took the departmental exam, I gave them a post-test as a comparison. Their results allowed me to make flexible groups or pair struggling students with peers who had less trouble. If appropriate for your course, find ways to pretest students' knowledge about a unit or topic.

Issue #4: Communicate Expectations and Feedback

The co-founder of Intel, Andy Grove, once said, "How well we communicate is determined not by how well we say things, but by how well we are understood." In other words, we need to meet the audience on their terms, not ours. In fact, *teacher clarity* was ranked 13th out of 195 in terms of factors that influence student learning, ahead of *teacher expectations* (77th), *classroom management* (53rd), and even *teaching strategies* (28th) in one study.[139] Students value instructors who are clear, especially when it comes to assignment requirements.[140] We need to manage their expectations through communication.

This goes back to teacher preparation. During the first year teaching my math methodology course, I assigned students to write reflection papers detailing what they observed in K–5 classrooms. Each week was devoted to a different topic—teacher-student interactions, classroom management techniques, etc. I specifically wanted them to also connect what they observed with ideas and concepts from the text or from class discussions. Yet their papers were wildly different in quality. Some students detailed only what they saw ("I saw [ABC]," I observed [XYZ]," etc.), with little reflection. Others described how their experiences influenced their perspective on teaching. Still others focused on one or two particular incidents in the classroom. Most did not make connections as I had asked.

Through my end-of-the semester feedback survey (for details on how to develop one, see *Issue #3: Are Your Students Really Learning?* earlier in this chapter), I found that students simply weren't clear on the assignment, even though I thought it was explained quite clearly in the syllabus:

Observation Topic #2: Teacher/Student Interaction. Is there evidence that the teacher demonstrates a good rapport with and respect for students and that s/he expects mutual respect among students? Are children intellectually engaged in the discussions, tasks, or activities? Is there evidence that the teacher is teaching in ways that specifically target the needs of specific individual children and groups of children with similar needs? Make connections to ideas and concepts from the readings and/or class discussions.

Actually, the description looked pretty clear to me. Yet it took me a while to realize that students don't exactly know what it means to *make connections.* They "kinda" know, but not really. That was when I realized the power of *exemplars*—or samples students can refer to (such as an effectively written paper, a model design, or a clear solution to a problem). Exemplars are not templates, which are about plugging responses into the blanks. More than anything, exemplars manage students' expectations by showing an example of how students have done the assignment from previous semesters (no names are ever used). I may highlight on a slide, for instance, why this particular student's paragraph worked. I also show different examples of how others have connected what they observed with what they've read. Concrete examples help students recognize what is expected. And when students understand, they will put in the time and effort to meet those expectations.[141]

On the flip side, I also show students what I do *not* want. This might be in the form of an anonymous paper that shows oversimplified thinking or a video that demonstrates errors. Reviewing common misinterpretations or showing both high- and low-quality work provides students with structure and, again, manage their expectations.

If you're teaching a course for the first time, you may have to create your own exemplars. Using previous students' work is more authentic, however. The key is to show excerpts of parts that will potentially give students the most trouble. *But aren't you giving students the answer?* you might ask. No. I am finding ways to help my students succeed—particularly the ones who need structure. Besides, assignments like this will differ from student to student, since they each have varied experiences.

I know it's less work to simply have students read the assignment requirements on their own. But the quality of work turned in *vastly improves* when exemplars are used. Students will appreciate the clarity.

Here are two other ways to manage expectations:

1. Model how you "think out loud." In elementary school classrooms, teachers frequently model math problem solving strategies through "think alouds." As students observe, the teacher describes how he or she approaches a problem ("So by reading the problem I can see that this requires multiple steps … I noticed that both fractions have different denominators …"). The teacher continues to narrate, sometimes posing himself or herself questions ("Wait a minute, is there an alternate way to solve this?"). The point is to act as a reference for students when they confront future tasks or problems. Education researcher Susan Ambrose and colleagues recommend getting students to use a series of questions to ask themselves, such as: *How would you begin? What steps would you take next? How would you know if your strategy is working? Is there an alternative (or more efficient) approach?*

2. *Rubrics* are documents that articulate the expectations for an assignment and typically range from 1 (poor) to 4 (excellent). University departments increasingly expect faculty to either incorporate rubrics into their syllabi or provide them for each assignment. Like exemplars, they give students a clear idea of what their work should be like. Unlike exemplars, however, rubrics provide conceptual guidelines rather than a concrete example.

Sample Rubric for Journal Evaluations

Outcome Assessed	Beginning 1	Developing 2	Proficient 3	Strong 4	Score
Overall	Entries are few and generally simple retellings or simple comments regarding topic.	Includes nearly all entries in response to prompts, but depth of exploration is limited.	Includes all required entries and thoughtful comments related to prompts.	Includes many entries with consistent, thorough, and thoughtful exploration of concepts.	
Intellectual engagement with key concepts	Makes no reference to issues raised through readings and/or class activities.	Makes some reference to issues raised through readings and class activities. Attempts to comprehend key concepts.	Demonstrates awareness of the key issues raised through readings and/or class activities. Attempts to apply key concepts.	Demonstrates engagement with the important issues raised through readings and/or class activities. Demonstrates analysis and application of key concepts.	
Personal response to key concepts	No personal response is made to the issues or concepts raised in readings and/or class activities.	Conveys little evidence of a personal response to the issues or concepts raised in the readings or class activities.	Conveys evidence of a personal response to the issues raised in the readings or class activities. Demonstrates capability of reflecting on learning, teaching, and future experience.	Conveys extensive evidence of a personal response to the issues raised in the readings and/or class activities. Demonstrates growth through reflection on learning, teaching, and future experiences.	

Since students are continually improving, developmental scales (with labels like "beginning," "developing," and "mastering") are worth using. They work well for both written as well as non-written assignments (e.g., presentations, self-assessment for students, and group work).

See the resources section for rubrics (including templates and ways to create them online) at the end of this book.

Next, let's talk about (written) feedback. How do you communicate it properly so it helps students? Ideally you want to include five elements:

1. What the student did well/right
2. What the student did incorrectly/wrong
3. Whether the student met the objective
4. What the student can do better
5. What the instructor can do to help him or her get better

Often, it is easy to jump right into constructive criticism (element #4)—meaning, the ways students can improve their work. However, they appreciate when teachers recognize strengths and effort. In fact, "warm" comments will make criticism easier to take in. Too many negative, or "cool," comments can demotivate. Note that elements #3 (meeting the objective) and 5 (ways the teacher can help) aren't always easy to do or feasible. Tailor them to your situation.

Below is one example of written feedback using all five elements (the "ideal" version) and a similar version using only three elements (the abridged, or what I call the "practical" version). I've numbered the type of feedback in brackets, as reference. Here, the student did an oral presentation on technology in the classroom.

Ideal: *Jin, your presentation demonstrates your ability to effectively engage students [3]. You grabbed their attention with an intriguing, relatable question ("How many times per hour do you check your text messages or social media?") [1]. You used an animated video to spur a class debate on the pros and cons of using technology in the classrooms. At times, however, students were talking over each other, which makes it hard to listen [2]. To improve, manage the process. This means calling on those patiently raising their hands or those who've yet to contribute—everyone is accountable [4]! I know this is hard because you said you felt nervous. To improve your confidence, watch Amy Cuddy's TED Talk on YouTube, called "Your Body Language Shapes Who You Are" [5]. This twenty-minute video may change how you feel about public speaking.*

<u>Practical</u>: *Jin, your presentation was solid. You grabbed the class's attention with an intriguing, relatable question ("How many times per hour do you check your text messages or social media?") [1]. You used a video to spur a class debate on the pros and cons of using technology in the classroom. At times, however, students were talking over each other, which makes it hard to listen [2]. To improve, you must manage the process. This means calling on those who are patiently raising their hands or those who have yet to contribute [4].*

Specificity helps students improve their work. Truthfully, however, I've been guilty of writing "Excellent insights!" when too many papers come across my desk. Incorporating the various elements of feedback is not easy when you teach many students. But they will appreciate it.

Issue #5: How Do I Get Students to Participate [More]?

Have you ever asked a question to the class, only to get zero responses? Does your class seem reticent? In my experience, students hesitate to participate for five main reasons:

1. They don't care.
2. They don't feel comfortable talking/sharing.
3. They feel they aren't expected to participate (they're used to the status quo).
4. They don't know the answer.
5. The question is complicated/you're not clear.

If students don't care, you have to find ways to relate the lesson to their concerns, perspectives and lives (see Chapter 5, *Develop Your Topic* and Chapter 6, *"Touch" Your Audience*).

Students who don't feel comfortable sharing or feel they aren't expected to participate (reasons #2–3) may feel the environment isn't quite safe or supportive. If you've cultivated the right environment, however (something else we discussed at the top of this chapter), students will open up.

When students don't know the answer or when the question is complicated (reasons #4–5), you can remedy this using four proven K–12 strategies.

Implement "wait time." With complicated questions, most teachers don't give students enough time to think. They give maybe two or three seconds before calling on the first raised hand (what my editor calls the "Hermione effect"). Yet quick answers are, as educator trainer Doug Lemov says in *Teach Like a Champion*, unlikely to be the richest, the most reflective, or the most developed responses. Calling the first participant also reinforces a non-participatory environment. Students are masters at doing that because they (we!) learned to do this since grade school.

Some students also process slower than others. Unfortunately, calling on the first hand gives the illusion that the class "gets it." Trust me—they don't.

To get more students to participate, K–12 teachers practice "wait time." Waiting ten seconds or longer may seem long and even agonizing. You may yearn to fill that gap. Avoid it, unless it's to clarify or encourage. Prompt them by saying things like, "Take ten seconds, go back to the text, and find it."[*] Normalizing a period of time after your question forces students to think. Wait time can improve the number of students raising their hands, and the number of students actively participating and actively *learning*. It really does work.

Sometimes, students just don't get what you're asking. My first instinct when students aren't raising their hands is to ask myself, "Is there an easier way to phrase this question?" Or, I might break the question down to smaller chunks: "OK, let's think about the first step only. What would you do first?"

---

[*] As one teacher said in a transcript from Lemov (2015), p. 248.

Ask students to turn and talk to a partner. With particularly complex or hard questions, I rely on two other widely known (and interrelated) K–12 techniques: *turn-and-talk* and *think–pair–share*.

With *turn-and-talk*, I ask students to turn to someone sitting next to them and discuss the answer. This reduces the pressure for students to explicate in front of the class while collaborating. Moreover, reluctant participants and/or quiet students get involved. Here's how you might incorporate it:

"Class, is there a difference between being *talented* at something versus being *intelligent*? What do you think? [Wait for a period of time.] Do me a favor: turn and talk to a partner and discuss for two minutes."

Notice the somewhat specific use of time frame, which signals that time is being monitored. It also manages students' expectations. Without parameters, students are left wondering, *For how long? Do I have forty-five seconds or ten minutes?* They don't know if this should be a deep conversation with multiple back-and-forth turns or a fairly quick endeavor.

Also, in my experience, anything longer than a few minutes of turn-and-talk is probably too long unless it is part of a larger brainstorm or writing activity, or it is a scenario-based problem. For straightforward questions, students will have exhausted their ideas after a few minutes. Too much time can lead to off-task behavior such as checking text messages, talking off topic, etc.

When done, students can share. You will notice higher

participation rates. Turn-and-talk is my go-to move when I sense students hesitating to answer.

Think-pair-share is similar. When asked a question, students think individually first (usually a couple of minutes or so). Here they can jot down some notes. Then, they pair up with a partner (or a small group) to discuss what they came up with. Finally, they share their responses with the class. This technique encourages students to think deeply and critically. *Think-pair-share* also helps them organize their thoughts.

Now ask yourself: Why is there a need to think individually before pairing? Time alone holds students accountable for their own thinking. It's easy for one party to rely on the other(s) to do the thinking. More importantly, you want to give slower-thinking students (as well as passive learners and/or non-native speakers) time to come up individually with solutions or responses, which they can then share with their partner/group. Without the individual element, fast-thinking students often "swallow" their slower counterparts.[142] *Think–pair–share* draws out immigrant students' participation in particular.

You don't need a lot of prep time to institute this. Here's one way to start (after you've posed the question/problem):

"We're going to do what's known as a *think–pair–share*. First, you're going to spend two minutes jotting down your thoughts. Then, I'll ask you to discuss with a neighbor for two minutes— this will help you expand your perspective and think critically.

You may decide to add or amend your notes at this point. Finally, we'll share your perspective."

Cold calling, a technique popularized in charter schools, ensures that students participate. If getting students to participate feels like pulling teeth, this technique will help. The rule: *Call on students regardless of whether they raised their hand.* Random selection eliminates the "If-I-don't-raise-my-hand-my-professor-won't-call-on-me" tactic so many students rely on.

Educator Doug Lemov considers cold calling the single best technique to improve the rigor and expectation level in a classroom. [143] It allows instructors to check for student understanding, create a culture of engaged accountability, manage the pacing of the lesson, and ensure high participation ratio. Ironically, cold calling helps students feel more comfortable participating and creates an environment that makes them *want* to participate more.[144] Participation begets more participation.

I see cold calling as a technique where I direct relatively straightforward questions to students:

"What do you think Piaget meant by *object permanence*? Viktor?"

"Anissa, can you think of examples of how *you* might be giving off *social cues*?"

Four things to consider when cold calling:

1. It must be done in good faith and not as a way to catch

disengaged students.

2. Cold calling *must* be used regularly to establish a culture where participation is expected.

3. Questions used with cold calls should be relatively uncomplicated so that students can answer without extended thinking time.

4. You need to know your students' names (see "Establish the Right Culture [and Impression] the First Day" near the beginning of this chapter).

As such, I tend to use cold calling for questions that are closed (one answer only or yes/no responses) or opinion-based. This pushes students to expect they will be called at any time. That is why cold calling must be regularly deployed. Without this consistency, it may surprise students who feel ambushed, caught off-guard, and resentful. (The worst thing to do is call on someone who wasn't paying attention—shaming them never works. Instead, discreetly tap their desk when passing by—yes, break the plane—or talk to them privately after class.)

Watch this example of cold calling in a 7th grade classroom:
"Mr. Rector's seventh grade class, as he uses Cold Call
Technique, with voiceover by Doug Lemov" (1:45) on YouTube.
Look past the structured way this teacher deploys this
technique and think about *how it can be modified for your*
classroom.

What happens when a student doesn't know (or have) the answer?

Often, students understand that if they say, "I don't know," the teacher will move on to someone who does know, which undermines their motivation to participate. The best way to address this is to move on to other students, listen to their responses, and then *go back to the first student and ask him/her to paraphrase.* Here's an example:

1. Instructor: "Shawn, how might *income* affect *achievement?*"

2. Shawn: "Um ... I don't know."

3. Instructor: "Can someone help Shawn out? Priyanka?"

4. Priyanka: "I think when you're poor, you might have less books and less money to go to places to learn—like museums, traveling, and science camp. Rich kids can do those things and they learn a lot."

5. Instructor: "Shawn, what do you think of Priyanka's response?"

6. Shawn: "I think she's right."

7. Instructor: "How so?"

8. Shawn: "I grew up in a school where a lot of people didn't have money. They never went to science camp or traveled. Their grades weren't so good ..."

By the way, I can modify my question in Line 5 in other ways:

"Shawn, can you repeat what she said?"

"Shawn, does that make sense? Can you paraphrase what she said?"

"Shawn, what other ways might poverty hurt achievement?"

Notice how the rigor increases with each question, depending on the instructor's confidence in Shawn's abilities. The first one only requires Shawn to parrot what his classmate said, which holds him accountable for listening. This is the very least he can do. The other two can be used to give Shawn a chance to build off of Priyanka's response while building his confidence to contribute meaningfully.

The point is to *always go back to the original student and hold them accountable for an answer.* Letting the student go without answering—even once or twice—signals to him (and the rest of the class) that 1) they aren't *required* to listen actively and vigilantly; and 2) they can remain uninvolved, or only involved sporadically. On the other hand, consistently going back to the student cultivates the expectation that *all* students need to contribute. *Repeating, rephrasing,* and *building off* are great K–12 strategies professors can use to help the unresponsive.

Speaking of building off, *follow-on* is a technique that flows from *cold calling* and socializes students to continue the conversation, add on, or give their perspective. It could be simple, such as, "May, do you agree with Jian Hui?" or more extensive: "Marcus, what are your thoughts about what Sandy said?" Follow-on reinforces an "always listening, always ready" expectation during discussions.[145] Again, there is no need to wait for students to raise their hands. Simply call on a new person to continue the line of thought from the previous participant.

When done regularly from day one, cold calling and follow-on can powerfully change the way students participate. But, make no mistake, their effectiveness depends on how consistently they are deployed. The more you use these techniques, the more students will participate.

What should you do when students ramble or go off topic?

We all know when usually well-meaning students over-share or bring up "this one time I _____." Although deep, insightful participation is encouraged, it can divert from the lesson when off-topic and, more importantly, frustrate peers who feel time is being wasted. One of students' biggest complaints is when teachers don't intervene on behalf of rambling peers, according to student interviews.[146] I've seen classmates who sigh or roll their eyes when a certain student starts going off on a tangent. Nothing is more frustrating. The best way is to cut him or her off nicely and directly. Any of the following phrases will work:

"Pause for a minute."

"Pause there."

"Stop for a minute."

"Hold on a sec."

"Wait."

"I'm going to stop you right there."

The key is to positively—but unapologetically—redirect their talk back to the lesson. For example:

"OK, Elliot, pause there. So you're saying that race and class have little to do with achievement? Anyone else?"

"Wait. Tie this back to our discussion on the roots of democracy."

"Hold on. You mentioned your grandparents' experiences growing up. Let's focus on that for a minute ... [then redirect]."

"Pause for a sec. What Janelle said reminds me of ... [redirect back to topic]."

By the way, I often use the response "I'm going to stop you right there" when the student is talking about an individual issue that has less to do with the class. For instance, if you are talking about the requirements for a research paper assignment, and a student asks a question relating to his or her specific topic ("My paper is about Montessori schools, and I'm having trouble …"), then you might say, "So listen, I'm going to stop you right there, OK? Since this is an individual issue, come talk to me after class." This lets others know that class time is valuable and should be used for the benefit of the whole. In an attempt to be thorough and/or helpful, instructors sometimes fail to consider the class's time.

Finally, keep in mind that talking is but one way to participate. There are other ways to engage the materials outside of whole class discussions/lectures, whether that be online discussion boards, one-on-one conversations with the instructor (email or office meetings), or small group/paired discussions. I encourage making this explicit to the class.

Wrap-Up

At the heart of good teaching is helping students succeed. This starts by recognizing their attitudes, struggles, doubts, and perspectives—the mindset that marketers adopt to understand their target audience. Have you actually thought about what keeps them up at night? What they juggle every day? What they want out of your course and their program? Do you remember what it was like to listen to boring lectures day after day as an undergraduate? Chances are, you don't remember much. But you do remember the instructors you learned from most.

I've been humbled when former students tell me this. Or when they email me years later asking me how I'm doing and give me updates on their life. One girl I taught in fifth grade coincidentally— out of all the colleges and classes she could have enrolled in—landed in my undergraduate class. Someone who, to this day, I still keep in touch with. That's the power of teaching effectively. You change someone's life.

FINAL THOUGHTS

Teaching college students is not much different from teaching those in K–12, as I have suggested earlier in the book. Why? Because teaching is inherently about *communicating* and *connecting*. Learning won't happen without either. This means putting yourself in the shoes of students and understanding their mindset, including their frustrations and needs. Marketers have long recognized that it's not about *you*. It's about the *customer*, the student—the one being serviced. It's about building trust and relationships. We as higher education faculty may hold the advanced degree, but that has little to do with our ability to communicate or connect.

The problem comes when we think we know everything. And let's be honest, it's hard not to think that way sometimes, especially when others think that way about us ("Hey, he's a PhD!"). Yet most people, including those who graduated from college, don't know their professors never learned how to teach. They just assume we have; after all, isn't that what we do for a living? So the illusion continues: we convince ourselves we can teach, and they believe it too.

That's why I'm forever grateful to have had the opportunity to learn from some of the best. My years as a marketer and a K–12 educator powerfully shaped my mindset as a higher education instructor. I've had colleagues at every level who inspire students in ways I can only dream of doing. I can only observe and imitate.

Teaching also humbles me. Students are forever saying and doing things that I don't have answers to. Like the freshman who confided in me that his traditional-minded parents wanted to throw him out because he admitted he was gay. Or the stressed-out undergraduate working a full-time job and taking five courses because taking less is *not* an option.

That's when I learn to listen. To deal with the students where they are, not where they should be. In this way, our real purpose as teachers is revealed: to guide. And sometimes, academics just isn't the priority. Listening to students is.

I'm reminded of what one Native Alaskan educator once said (as cited by education scholar Lisa Delpit): "In order to teach you, I must know you."[147] In the end, that's what the marketing and K–12 mentality boils down to. This idea is the heart of *Teaching College*.

Thank you,

Norman Eng

APPENDICES

Note: Purchasers of this book can download the following templates
FREE at
http://NormanEng.org/downloadable-templates
(Type in the password: teachingcollegetemplates)

Appendix A
Teaching Your Students to Present, Part 1:
"Understanding the Psychology of Presenting" Lesson Plan

Appendix B
Teaching Your Students to Present, Part 2:
The Three-Step Roadmap

Appendix C
Lecture-Driven Interactive Lessons:
Guideline/Template

Appendix D
Activity-Driven Interactive Lessons:
Guideline/Template
(the *You, Y'all, We* Approach)

Appendix E
Exit Ticket Template

Appendix F
Student Feedback Survey Template

APPENDIX A

Teaching Your Students to Present, Part 1:
"Understanding the Psychology of Presenting" Lesson Plan[148]

Learning Objective

Students will know the difference between a *content-focused* and a *learner-centered* approach by examining prior experiences with presentations and lectures.

Grade Level: Undergraduate (or graduate) education students
Length: 45 minutes
Materials: None needed

InTASC (Interstate Teacher Assessment and Support Consortium) Standards

Standard 1: Learner Development. The teacher understands how learners grow and develop, recognizing that patterns of learning and development vary individually within and across the cognitive, linguistic, social, emotional, and physical areas, and designs and implements developmentally appropriate and challenging learning experiences.

Standard 5: Application of Content. The teacher understands how to connect concepts and use differing perspectives to engage learners in critical thinking, creativity, and collaborative problem solving relating to authentic local and global issues.

Pre-Activity (15–20 minutes)

Start by asking candidates about their prior experiences with class presentations or lectures, such as: "What makes presentations bad?" or "Why are some lectures boring?"

Solicit answers. If needed, have students turn and talk to each other first to draw out participation. Answers will likely touch on some of following reasons:

1. Presentation/Lecture is too long
2. Information presented is too dense
3. Presenters/Lecturers read directly from slides or notes
4. Presenters/Lecturers do not connect with or involve audience

Use these reasons to establish the primary role of teachers, which is *to help students learn through meaningful experiences*. It is not to deliver content or convey knowledge per se, as many may believe. For instance, you might say, "Based on your reasons, it seems that many lectures and presentations are bad because they convey information that doesn't relate to the class. So, what might good teachers do instead?

The purpose is to help candidates understand that teaching focuses on *the needs of the learner* (what's known as the student-centered or learner-centered approach), which entails concrete experiences. Ask candidates what kinds of activities or tasks they might use to engage students. Write down their responses on the board. Responses may include: discussions, surveys, debates, group activities, quizzes, and games.

Activity (15 minutes)

In groups, candidates will apply the content-focused approach and the learner-centered approach to a specific topic, such as the American Civil War, Albert Einstein, How to write an essay, or any general topic (avoid education-specific topics, as most may not have taken education courses). Prompt them with the following questions: "How might you have presented this topic *before*? How would you present this topic *now* as a teacher?" The point is two help candidates crystallize the difference between the two approaches. Each group should select a representative to share their ideas with the class.

Post-Activity (10 minutes)

Have each group share their ideas with the class. Reinforce the importance of a learner-centered approach through open-ended questions and discussions (e.g., "Why might this idea help students learn more?").

APPENDIX B

Teaching Your Students to Present, Part 2:

The Three-Step Roadmap

Step 1: "Niche Down" Your Topic

Niche down means to narrow your topic. You do *not* want to present or teach the whole article—just the most important things. In fact, do not even rehash the assigned reading! If you find yourself repeating the details of the reading, the audience will be bored.

Instead, find one or two (maybe three) important things in your topic to teach. One way to think about this is to ask yourself: *What thing(s) do my students need to know MOST about this topic?*

For example, if my topic is John Dewey (a famous educator), I would narrow it down to his most important contribution: He believed that *experience* is the best way for children to learn, not passive listening. Therefore, teachers need to create active, hands-on experiences. So that's what I will focus on: teaching the class about the importance of "experiential learning."

YOUR TURN: Write at least one or two major things you will focus on from the reading:

1. _____

2. _____ (if necessary)

3. _____ (if necessary)

Step 2: Make Your Topic Relevant

Now that you niched down your topic, let's make it relevant to your audience. Remember, teaching is not simply about conveying knowledge. It is about *creating experiences that help students learn and grow*, as Dewey believed. To make your presentation meaningful, ask yourself the four following questions (do your best to answer):

1. Why is this topic (or concept or idea) important for education students to know? (Example of answer: Dewey's experiential learning is important because students learn best when they are actively participating.)

2. How is this topic relevant (or meaningful) to your audience? (Example: Experiential learning is relevant because future teachers need to know how to create meaningful experiences to engage their audience.)

3. How can you make this topic or idea easier to understand? (Examples: I might use a short video I found online that captures Dewey's idea of experiential learning. I might also ask the audience if they've ever been bored in class and *why*. I might have them try to brainstorm activities that will engage their future students. I might tell a story about the one time I fell asleep in history class and the teacher caught me! That will engage my audience *and* lead into my lesson on experience-based learning.)

4. How can you *apply* this topic or idea to real life? In other words, help students use this in their life. (Example: I will make sure to

involve my audience in hands-on learning. I might give them a specific topic—like the Civil War—and have them brainstorm in groups two ways to approach teaching this lesson—a traditional way and a hands-on way.)

YOUR TURN: Jot your answers to these questions.

Step 3: Flesh Out Your Lesson

It's time to actually create your presentation lesson! There are four parts: *opening*, *mini-lesson*, *activity*, and *summary*. Use what you wrote in Steps 1 and 2 to help you write your 15- to 25-minute lesson.

Opening (1–5 minutes)

Grabbing your audience's attention in the beginning is critical because it sets the tone for the whole lesson. The opening must be motivating, interesting, and relevant to your topic. Here are some ideas.

- Ask a thought-provoking question (ex: "What is a *bad* presentation?")
- Bring up an interesting fact or statistic (ex: "Did you know that 60 percent of students get bored in school everyday?")
- Tell a relevant personal story or anecdote (ex: "When I was a high school student, I used to believe that …")
- Use a relevant quote or saying (ex: "There's a quote that says

'_____.' What do think that means?")

- Start with a warm-up activity for class (ex: "Raise your hands if you have ever …")

YOUR TURN: Which will you use? (You can also come up with your own ideas.)

Mini-lesson (5–10 minutes)

Here's where you teach your topic, concept, or idea(s). You may use lecture, slides, or something else. Remember to keep it focused on one or two things. Think about what your audience cares about. Incorporate videos, pictures, photos, illustrations, and questions!

YOUR TURN: Write details of what you are presenting on the back of this page.

Student Activity (10 minutes)

Incorporate one of the following activities:

- Surveys/questionnaires (written or asked out loud)
- Class discussion (use at least three open-ended questions)
- Debate (divide the class into two sides to debate an issue)
- Game (must be relevant, not just "fun")
- Quiz (make it fun and relevant, not just like a test)
- Role-playing (helps students understand something by playing a part)

- Group work (have small groups each work on one aspect of the topic and explain their findings to the class)

Be creative! You can even do something that's not on this list. If you're not sure what to do, I recommend group work since it involves everyone. Remember, activities are designed to deepen students' understanding of a topic.

Using my previous example of John Dewey, I might use group work and say, "Pretend you are teaching about the American Civil War. What kind of hands-on experiences would you use to help children learn? Break into groups of four. Brainstorm ideas and write them down. You have ten minutes."

Do you see how this activity helps the audience delve into John Dewey's idea of experiential learning? They aren't just learning his theory, but actively *applying* it. They're using it in a way that will help them when they become teachers. Your topic, no matter what it is, should find a way to help your classmates apply it to teaching. It will also help them remember your lesson so much more. That's what great teachers do.

I suggest keeping activities simple, especially if this is the first time you are teaching. Games like *Jeopardy!* are nice, but harder to manage.

YOUR TURN: Write down what activity (or activities) you are planning to incorporate. Be specific: Exactly how will it work?

How much time is needed? How many per group? How will it help them learn your topic more deeply? Detail it here:

Summary/Conclusion (1–5 minutes)

Wrap it up and tie it back to your opening. Re-emphasize the main point you want your students to learn: "So from now on when you are teaching, remember to …" Write on the back of this page.

APPENDIX C

Lecture-Driven Interactive Lessons:
Guideline/Template

Lesson Date: _____ Time: _____ to _____ Class length: _____

Broad Topic:

Title/Essential Question:

How can [insert your niche concept/idea here] *help you* [insert desired outcome]*?*

Why is [insert your niche concept/idea here] an *important part of* [insert a competency or skill]*?*

Why is [insert your niche concept/idea here] *important for* [insert students' potential career]*?*

Objective: Students will be able to:

What will they be able to do? *Students will ...*
How will they accomplish this? *By ...*
How does this benefit them? *So that ...*

Beginning (Pre-Activity)

<u>Opening</u>: What opening will immediately and appropriately engage students?
- Ask a thought-provoking question
- Bring up an interesting fact or statistic

- Tell a relevant story or anecdote
- Use a relevant quote or saying
- Start with an analogy (something students already know)
- Open with a warm-up activity
- Set the stage with a scenario

Lecture (use responses below to plan lecture)

a. What part of the topic will you focus on? (1–3 only)

b. Why is this topic/concept/idea important?

c. How can you make it relevant, meaningful, and/or easier to understand? (If possible, search for the underlying idea of the topic or the universal experience students can relate to.)

d. How can you apply this topic/concept/idea to a student's life?

e. How will you deliver your lecture? Will you use slides?

Guided Practice (if applicable; mainly for problem-solving courses, like STEM)

How will you help students practice what you have just taught? Will you pair students? How will you assess their understanding?

Turn-and-talk (with partner)

Middle (Activity)

What activity or activities will you use to deepen students' understanding? (Use more than one if possible)

- Discussion
- Debate/competition
- Small group work
- Surveys/inventories
- Role-play/perspective-taking
- Demonstration
- Oral presentations
- Case studies

End (Post-Activity)

How will you assess your students' understanding of today's topic/concept/idea(s)?

Reflect/Share
Exit ticket
Quiz/Answering essential question

Will this be done orally or written?

How will you tie the lesson back to the lesson objective or essential question?

Support

What are some obstacles you anticipate? How will you address them?

APPENDIX D

Activity-Driven Interactive Lessons:
Guideline/Template
(the *You, Y'all, We* Approach)

Lesson Date: _____ Time: _____ to _____ Class length: _____

Broad Topic:

Title/Essential Question:

> *How can* [insert your niche concept/idea here] *help you* [insert desired outcome]*?*
> *Why is* [insert your niche concept/idea here] *an important part of* [insert a competency or skill]*?*
> *Why is* [insert your niche concept/idea here] *important for* [insert students' potential career]*?*

Objective: Students will be able to:

> What will they be able to do? *Students will ...*
> How will they accomplish this? *By ...*
> How does this benefit them? *So that ...*

Beginning/Middle
(What will *You*—the student—do?)
(What will *Y'all*—as a group—do?)

> What dilemma, scenario, problem, or case study do you

immediately engage students to work on? May be done individually first or in groups. Describe below.

End (What will *We*—as a class—do?)

How will students share their work? What is the point to reinforce of the dilemma, scenario, problem, or case study?

Support

What are some obstacles you anticipate? How will you address them?

APPENDIX E

Exit Ticket Template

Exit Ticket	**Exit Ticket**
Name _____	Name _____
1. What is *multiple intelligence*?	1. What is *multiple intelligence*?
Exit Ticket	**Exit Ticket**
Name _____	Name _____
1. What is *multiple intelligence*?	1. What is *multiple intelligence*?

APPENDIX F

Student Feedback Survey Template

(Note: Brackets indicate areas that can be modified)

End of Semester Survey/[COURSE NUMBER]   [INSTRUCTOR NAME]

Part I. INSTRUCTION

1. How useful were the following instructional approaches to help you think about [YOUR DISCIPLINE]?

	Very useful		Useful		Not useful
[INSTRUCTOR LECTURES]	5	4	3	2	1
[ORAL PRESENTATIONS]	5	4	3	2	1
[OTHERS' PRESENTATIONS]	5	4	3	2	1
[CLASS DISCUSSIONS]	5	4	3	2	1
[SOCRATIC DISCUSSIONS]	5	4	3	2	1
[NAME GAME]	5	4	3	2	1

2. Which approach from above was *most useful*? Why? (You can list more than one)

3. Which approach, if any, was *not* as useful? Why?

Part II. ASSIGNMENTS

4. How useful were the following assignments to help you think about [YOUR DISCIPLINE]?

	Very useful		Useful	Not useful	
[PRESENTATIONS]	5	4	3	2	1
[READING ENTRIES]	5	4	3	2	1
[SEMINAR PREP GUIDE]	5	4	3	2	1
[FIELDWORK REPORTS]	5	4	3	2	1
[TERM PAPER]	5	4	3	2	1

5. Which assignment from above was *most useful*? Why? (You can list more than one)

6. Which assignment, if any, was *not* as useful? Why?

Part III. OVERALL COURSE

Circle one number for each question.

	Strongly Agree	Agree	Not Sure	Disagree	Strongly Disagree
7. It was useful to learn [ABC SKILL].	5	4	3	2	1
8. It was useful to learn. [XYZ SKILL]	5	4	3	2	1
9. I was able to voice my comments in class when I wanted to	5	4	3	2	1
10. Overall, [INSTRUCTOR]. provided useful written feedback on assignments	5	4	3	2	1

11. What did [INSTRUCTOR] do in general that makes this course helpful or useful? Please be specific.

12. What useful suggestion(s) for this course would you make to

help [INSTRUCTOR] teach future students? Please be honest.

13. In terms of instruction and assignments, how does this course *compare* with other [DISCIPLINE] courses? Please don't use names or describe personalities; just keep it in terms of instructional approach and assignments.

14. Rate this course overall on a scale from 1 through 10: _____
    10 = Very Useful
     1 = Not Useful

RESOURCES

(Listed by Chapter)

Chapter 3 Adopt an Active Approach

The Science of Learning

How Learning Works (2010), Susan Ambrose, Michael Bridges, Michele DiPietro, Marsha Lovett, Marie Norman

How People Learn: Brain, Mind, Experience, and School (2000):

FREE PDF: http://www.nap.edu/catalog/9853/how-people-learn-brain-mind-experience-and-school-expanded-edition

Make it Stick: The Science of Successful Learning (2014), Peter Brown, Henry Roediger III, Mark McDaniel

Active Learning

The Power of Problem-Based Learning: A Practical Guide for Teaching Undergraduate Courses in Any *Discipline*, Barbara Duch, Susan Groh, and Deborah Allen (Eds.) (2001).

Teaching and Learning STEM: A Practice Guide, Rich Felder and Rebecca Brent (2016)

Chapter 4 Start with Your Syllabus

Writing and Designing Your Syllabus

Links:

Best Practices *in Syllabus Writing: Contents of a Learner-Centered Syllabus* (Johnson, 2006):

http://www.ncbi.nlm.nih.gov/pmc/articles/PMC2384173/

Writing a Syllabus (Cornell):

https://www.cte.cornell.edu/teaching-ideas/designing-your-course/writing-a-syllabus.html

Creating a Syllabus (Stanford):

https://teachingcommons.stanford.edu/resources/course-preparation-resources/creating-syllabus

Books:

Teaching at Its Best: A Research-Based Resource for College Instructors (Nilson, L., 2010)

The Course Syllabus*: A Learning-Centered Approach* (O'Brien, J. & Millis, B., 2008)

Designing your syllabus:

Accessible Syllabus: https://accessiblesyllabus.tulane.edu

The Non-Designer's *Design Book*, 3rd ed. (Robin Williams, 2008)

A rubric to evaluate your syllabus:

https://www.cte.cornell.edu/documents/Syllabus%20Rubric.pdf

Chapter 6 "Touch" Your Audience

Case Studies

Teaching and the Case Method (Barnes, Christensen, & Hansen 1994)

Teaching with Cases: Learning to Question (Boehrer & Linsky, 1990)

Group Work or Assignments

Working in Groups: Derek Bok Center for Teaching and Learning, Harvard University:
http://isites.harvard.edu/fs/html/icb.topic58474/wigintro.html

Turning Student Groups into Effective Teams (including *Getting to Know You* form that forms basis for groups):
http://www4.ncsu.edu/unity/lockers/users/f/felder/public/Papers/Oakley-paper(JSCL).pdf

Jigsaw method: https://www.jigsaw.org/

Oral Presentation Guidelines for Students:
http://serc.carleton.edu/case/speaking.html

In-Class Debates:
http://www.isetl.org/ijtlhe/pdf/IJTLHE200.pdf

Demonstrations

Science Education Resource Center (SERC) at Carleton College:
http://serc.carleton.edu/sp/library/demonstrations/what.html

http://serc.carleton.edu/sp/library/demonstrations/how.html

Introductory Probability and Statistics (Gelman & Glickman, 2000):

http://www.stat.columbia.edu/~gelman/research/published/smiley12.pdf

Chapter 8 Use Slides as Support

Resources on Presentations:

Guide to making a PechaKucha presentation:
http://avoision.com/pechakucha

How to tell a story:
https://www.ted.com/playlists/62/how_to_tell_a_story

Deconstructing great presentations:
http://blog.hubspot.com/marketing/great-ted-talk-deconstructed-ht

Presenting *to Win*, by Jerry Weissman
TedTalks, by Chris Anderson
slide:ology: The Art and Science of Creating Great Presentations, by Nancy Duarte
Presentation Zen: Simple Ideas on Presentation *Design and Delivery*, by Garr Reynolds

Looking for Ideas, Pictures, Videos? Sharing Knowledge and Creativity Legally:

Creative Commons *in Education*:
https://creativecommons.org/about/program-areas/education-oer/education-oer-resources/

Creative Commons *search*: http://search.creativecommons.org

Chapter 9 Optimize Discussions and Activities

FREE PDF Guides:

Facilitating Discussion: *A Brief Guide* (Katherine Gottschalk, Cornell University):
http://www.arts.cornell.edu/knight_institute/publicationsprizes/Facilitating_Discussion06.pdf

Guidebook for Student-*Centered Classroom Discussions* (Jack Byrd Jr. and Suzanne Goodney Lea, Interactivity Foundation):
https://www.interactivityfoundation.org/wp-content/uploads/2009/12/Guidebook-for-Student-Centered-Classroom-Discussions.pdf

Classroom Discussions (Northern Illinois University, Faculty Development and Instructional Design Center):
http://www.niu.edu/facdev/_pdf/guide/strategies/classroom_discussions.pdf

Effective Classroom Discussions (William Cashin, Kansas State University): http://ideaedu.org/wp-content/uploads/2014/11/IDEA_Paper_49.pdf

Start Talking: A Handbook for Engaging in Difficult Dialogues in

the Classroom: http://www.difficultdialoguesuaa.org/handbook

Books

Classroom Communication: Collected Readings for Effective Discussion and Questioning (Rose Ann Neff and Maryellen Weimer [Editors], Atwood Publishing, 1989)

The Habit of Thought: From Socratic Seminars to Socratic Practice (Michael Strong, New View Publications, 1997)

Socratic Circles: Fostering Critical and Creative Thinking in Middle and High School. (Matt Copeland, Stenhouse, 2005)

Questioning for Classroom Discussion: Purposeful Speaking, Engaged Listening, Deep Thinking (Jackie Acree Walsh and Beth Dankert Sattes, Association for Supervision & Curriculum Development, 2015)

Chapter 10 Fix Lingering Issues

Promoting Student Engagement and Learning Environment
21 Teaching Strategies to Promote Student Engagement and Cultivate Classroom Equity:
http://ctl.yale.edu/sites/default/files/basic-page-supplementary-materials-files/tanner2013cbe_2013_equitystrategies.pdf

Cultivating a Safe Environment:
Active Learning: 101 Strategies to Teach Any Subject (Silberman, M., 1996)

500 Tips on Group Learning, Race P (2000)

*Diversity and Inclusion in the College Classroom (*Faculty Focus Special Report, 2016): http://www.facultyfocus.com/free-reports/diversity-and-inclusion-in-the-college-classroom/

Getting Students To Read
Getting Students to Read: 14 Tips:
http://ideaedu.org/wp-content/uploads/2014/11/Idea_Paper_40.pdf

11 Strategies for Getting Students to Read What's Assigned (2010):
https://www.canadacollege.edu/inside/CIETL/getting_students_to_read.pdf

Personal Response Systems (Clickers):
Teaching with Classroom Response Systems (Derek Bruff, 2009)

Free "Clicker"—using Google Forms:
Article #1: http://www.facultyfocus.com/articles/teaching-with-technology-articles/free-clickers-for-all-using-google-forms-to-survey-your-students/

Article #2: Guide to using classroom response systems:
https://cft.vanderbilt.edu/guides-sub-pages/clickers/

Using Clickers in the Classroom (VIDEO):
https://www.youtube.com/watch?v=CnnP0uCqD4k&feature=email

Non-technology response surveys

Creating a survey using Google Forms:
https://support.google.com/docs/answer/87809?hl=en

Getting to Know You Surveys
https://backtoschool.panoramaed.com/

Growth Mindset Lesson Plans and Videos
Growth Mindset Kit:
https://www.mindsetkit.org/static/files/YCLA_LessonPlan_v10.
pdf

Rubrics

Creating your own template:
- RubiStar: Create Rubrics for your Project-Based Learning Activities: http://rubistar.4teachers.org/index.php
- Word document: http://uwf.edu/media/university-of-west-florida/offices/cutla/documents/rubric-template.docx
- Quick Rubric: https://www.quickrubric.com/r#/create-a-rubric
- Annenberg Learner: Build a rubric: http://www.learner.org/workshops/hswriting/interactives/rubric/

View Rubric Samples:
- Valid Assessment of Learning in Undergraduate Education (VALUE) Rubric, by the Association of American Colleges and Universities' (AACU): http://www.aacu.org/value-rubrics
- Rubric for Online Discussion:

http://www.csuchico.edu/tlp/resources/rubric/rubric.pdf

- Poetry Reading and performance rubric: http://www.readwritethink.org/files/resources/lesson_images/lesson1001/poetry.pdf
- Rubric Library: http://www.fresnostate.edu/academics/oie/assessment/rubric.html
- Rubrics for (science) research paper, portfolio, reflective essay, lab report, oral presentation: https://www.cte.cornell.edu/documents/Science%20Rubrics.pdf
- Rubrics for Assessment (many areas): http://www.uwstout.edu/soe/profdev/rubrics.cfm
- E-Portfolio (Digital Portfolio) Rubric: https://www2.uwstout.edu/content/profdev/rubrics/eportfoliorubric.html

Learn more about Rubrics:
- Guide to Scoring Rubrics: http://www.opencolleges.edu.au/informed/teacher-resources/guide-to-scoring-rubrics/
- Scoring rubrics: What, When, and How? http://pareonline.net/getvn.asp?v=7&n=3
- Guide to Rating Critical and Integrative Thinking: http://www.cpcc.edu/learningcollege/learning-outcomes/rubrics/WST_Rubric.pdf

References

Allain, R. (2011, October 5). How to model Newton's cradle. *Wired.* Retrieved from https://www.wired.com/2011/10/how-to-model-newtons-cradle/

Allan, J., Clarke, K., and Jopling, M. (2009). Effective teaching in higher education: Perceptions of first year undergraduate students. *International Journal of Teaching and Learning in Higher Education, 21*(3), 362–372.

Ambrose, S. A., Bridges, M. W., DiPietro, M., Lovett, M. C., and Norman, M. K. (2010). *How learning works: 7 research-based principles for smart teaching.* San Francisco, CA: Jossey-Bass.

American Association for the Advancement of Science. (2011). *Vision and change in undergraduate biology education: A call to action [final report].* Washington, DC: Author.

American Association of University Professors (n.d.). *Background facts about contingent faculty.* Retrieved from https://www.aaup.org/issues/contingency/background-facts

Anderson, L. W., and Krathwohl, D. R. (Eds.) (2001). *A taxonomy for learning, teaching, and assessing: A revision of Bloom's taxonomy of educational objectives.* Boston, MA: Allyn & Bacon.

Andrews, T. M., Leonard, M. J., Colgrove, C. A., and Kalinowsky, S. T. (2011). Active learning not associated with student learning in a random sample of college biology courses. *CBE Life Sciences Education*, *10*(4), 394–405.

Angelo, T. A. and Cross, K. P. (1993). *Classroom assessment techniques: A handbook for college teachers.* San Francisco, CA: Jossey-Bass.

Arum, R., and Roksa, J. (2011). *Academically adrift: Limited learning on college campuses.* Chicago, IL: University of Chicago Press.

Atkinson, M. (2005). *Lend me your ears: All you need to know about making speeches and presentations.* New York: Oxford University Press.

Aronson, E., and Patnoe, S. (2011). *Cooperation in the classroom: The Jigsaw Method* (3rd ed.). London, UK: Pinter & Martin Ltd.

Bain, K. (2004). *What the best college teachers do.* Cambridge, MA: Harvard University Press.

Bakhtin, M. M. (1981). *The dialogic imagination: Four essays.* Austin and London: University of Texas Press.

Bargh, J. A., and Schul, Y. (1980). On the cognitive benefits of teaching. *Journal of Educational Psychology, 72*(5), 593–604.

Barone, J., Chaplinsky, C., Ehnle, T., Heaney, J., Jackson, R., Kaler, Z., Kossy, R., Lane, B., Lawrence, T., Lee, J., Lullo, S., McCammack, K., Seeder, D., Smith, C., and Wade, D. (2016, January 4). A lecture from the lectured. *Vitae.* Retrieved from https://chroniclevitae.com/news/1235-a-lecture-from-the-lectured

Bart, M. (2015, July 29). A learner-centered syllabus helps set the tone for learning. *Faculty Focus*. Retrieved from http://www.facultyfocus.com/articles/effective-classroom-management/a-learner-centered-syllabus-helps-set-the-tone-for-learning/

Birch, S. H., and Ladd, G. W. (1997). The teacher-child relationship and children's early school adjustment. *Journal of School Psychology*, *35*(1), 61–79.

Bligh, D. (1971). *What's the use of lectures?* San Francisco, CA: Jossey-Bass.

Boehrer, J., and Linsky, M. (1990). Teaching with cases: Learning to question. In M. D. Svinicki (ed.), The changing face of college teaching. *New Directions for Teaching and Learning*, 42. San Francisco: Jossey-Bass.

Bruff, D. (2015, September 15). *In defense of continuous exposition by the teacher* [web log post]. Retrieved from http://derekbruff.org/?p=3126

Budesheim, T., and Lundquist, A. (2000). Consider the opposite: Opening minds through in-class debates on course-related controversies. *Teaching of Psychology, 26*(2), 106–110.

Burchfield, C. M., and Sappington, J. (2000). Compliance with required reading assignments. *Teaching of Psychology, 27*(1), 58–60.

Burns, R. A. (1985, May). *Information impact and factors affecting recall.* Paper presented at the annual National Conference on Teaching Excellence and Conference of Administrators, Austin, TX. (ERIC Document Reproduction Service No. ED 258 639).

CareerBuilder. (2015). *Companies planning to hire more recent college graduates this year and pay them better, according to CareerBuilder survey.* Chicago, IL: Author. Retrieved from http://www.careerbuilder.com/share/aboutus/pressreleasesdet ail.aspx?sd=4%2f23%2f2015&siteid=cbpr&sc_cmp1=cb_pr88 9_&id=pr889&ed=12%2f31%2f2015

Carolyn Works. (2009, November 7). *Why learning from PowerPoint lectures is frustrating* [Web log post]. Retrieved from http://blog.carolynworks.com/?p=154

Chambliss, D. F. (2014, August 26). Learn your students' names. *Inside Higher Ed.* Retrieved from https://www.insidehighered.com/views/2014/08/26/essay-calling-faculty-members-learn-their-students-names

Chesler, M., Wilson, M., and Malani, A. (1993). *Perceptions of faculty behavior by students of color. The Michigan Journal of Political Science, 16,* 54–79.

Council for Aid to Education (2014). *CLA+ national results, 2013 – 14* [report]. New York: Author. Retrieved from http://cae.org/images/uploads/pdf/CLA_National_Results_2 013-14.pdf

Cron, L. (2012). *Wired for story: The writer's guide to using brain science to hook readers from the very first sentence.* Berkeley, CA: Ten Speed Press.

Crouch, C. H., Fagen, A. P., Callan, J. P., and Mazur, E. (2004). Classroom demonstrations: Learning tools or entertainment? *American Journal of Physics, 72*(6) 835–38.

Dallimore, E. J., Hertenstein, J. H., and Platt, M. B. (2013). Impact of cold-calling on student voluntary participation. *Journal of Management Education, 37*(3), 305–341.

Delpit, L. (1995). *Other people's children: Cultural conflict in the classroom.* New York: New Press.

DeSurra, C. J., and Church, K. A. (1994). *Unlocking the classroom closet: Privileging the marginalized voices of gay/lesbian college students.* Paper presented at the Annual Meeting of the Speech Communication Association. Retrieved from http://files.eric.ed.gov/fulltext/ED379697.pdf

Downey, M. (2016, June 2). *What teens resent: Classrooms controlled by students rather than teachers* [web log post]. Retrieved from http://getschooled.blog.myajc.com/2016/06/02/what-teens-resent-classrooms-controlled-by-students-rather-than-teachers/

Duarte, N. (2008). *slide:ology: The art and science of creating great presentations.* Sebastopol, CA: O'Reilly Media, Inc.

Duch, B. J., Groh, S. E., and Allen, D. E. (Eds.) (2001). *The power of problem-based learning: A practical guide for teaching undergraduate courses in any discipline.* London, UK: Falmer/KP.

Duhigg, C. (2016). *Smarter faster better: The secrets of being productive in life and business.* New York: Random House.

Dweck, C. (2006). *Mindset: The new psychology of success.* New York: Random House.

Dweck, (2015, September 22). Growth mindset, revisited [Commentary]. *Education Week, 35*(5), 20, 24.

Eagan, M. K., Stolzenberg, E. B., Berdan Lozano, J., Aragon, M. C., Suchard, M. R., and Hurtado, S. (2014). *Undergraduate teaching faculty: The 2013–2014 HERI Faculty Survey.* Los Angeles: Higher Education Research Institute, UCLA.

Eddy, S., and Hogan, K. (2014). "Getting under the hood: How and for whom does increasing course structure work?" *Cell Biology Education (CBE) Life Sciences Education. 13*(3), 453–468.

Eddy, S., Brown, S., and Wenderoth, M. (2014). Gender gaps in achievement and participation in multiple introductory biology classrooms. *CBE Life Sciences Education, 13*(3), 478–492.

Eng, N. (2016). *The potential of early practice: A case study,* presented at the American Educational Research Association Conference, Washington, D.C., 2016.

Finley, T. (2016, July 27). *9 ways to plan transformational lessons:*

Planning the best curriculum unit ever [web log post].
Retrieved from Edutopia: http://www.edutopia.org/blog/9-
ways-plan-transformational-lessons-todd-finley

Fisher, D., Frey, N., and Rothenberg, C. (2008). *Content-area
conversations: How to plan discussion-based lessons for diverse
language learners.* Alexandria, VA: Association for
Supervision and Curriculum Development.

Flanders, N. (1970). *Analyzing teacher behavior.* Reading, MA:
Addison-Wesley.

Foote, S. (2010). Amateur hour beginning in the lecture hall.
Pedagogy, 10(3), 457–470.

Foran, J. (2001). The case method and the interactive classroom.
Thought and Action, 17(1), 41–50.

Fosnot, C. T. (1996). Constructivism: A psychological theory of
learning. In C. T. Fosnot (ed.), *Constructivism: Theory,
perspectives, and practice* (pp. 8–33). New York: Teachers
College Press.

Freeman, S., Eddy, S. L., McDonough, M., Smith, M. K.,
Okoroafor, N., Jordt, H., and Wenderoth, M. P. (2014).
Active learning increases student performance in science,
engineering, and mathematics. *Proceedings of the National
Academy of Sciences of the United States of America, 111*(23),
8410–8415. Retrieved from
http://www.pnas.org/content/111/23/8410

Friedman, T. (2013, March 31). Need a job? Invent it. *The New York Times*, SR11. Retrieved from http://www.nytimes.com/2013/03/31/opinion/sunday/friedman-need-a-job-invent-it.html

Fruscione, J. (2014, July 25). When a college contracts "adjunctivitis," it's the students who lose. *PBS Newshour*. Retrieved from http://www.pbs.org/newshour/making-sense/when-a-college-contracts-adjunctivitis-its-the-students-who-lose/

Fryer, B. (2003). Storytelling that moves people. *Harvard Business Review*. Retrieved from https://hbr.org/2003/06/storytelling-that-moves-people

Gage, N. L. (ed.). (1976). *The psychology of teaching methods: The seventy-fifth yearbook of the National Society for the Study of Education*. Chicago: University of Chicago Press.

Gawande, A. (2013, July 29). Slow ideas: Some innovations spread fast. How do you speed the ones that don't? *The New Yorker*. Retrieved from http://www.newyorker.com/magazine/2013/07/29/slow-ideas

Gehlbach, H. and Robinson, C. (2016). *Creating birds of a feather: The potential of similarity to connect teachers and students*. Retrieved from American Enterprise Institute website: http://www.aei.org/wp-content/uploads/2016/08/Creating-

Birds-of-a-Feather.pdf

Gelman, A., and Glickman, M. E. (2000). Some class-participation demonstrations for introductory probability and statistics. *Journal of Educational and Behavioral Statistics, 25*(1), 84–100. Retrieved from http://www.stat.columbia.edu/~gelman/research/published/smiley12.pdf

Godin, S. (n.d.). *Really bad PowerPoint (and how to avoid it)* [ebook]. Retrieved from http://www.sethgodin.com/freeprize/reallybad-1.pdf

Goffe, W. L., and Kauper, D. (2014). A survey of principles instructors: Why lecture prevails. *Journal of Economic Education. 45*(4), 360–375.

Gonzalez, J. (2015, July 23). Icebreakers that rock [web log post]. *Cult of Pedagogy*. Retrieved from http://www.cultofpedagogy.com/classroom-icebreakers/

Goodman, A. (2006). *Why bad presentations happen to good causes: And how to ensure they won't happen to yours.* Los Angeles, CA: Cause Communications.

Green, C., and Klug, H. (1990). Teaching critical thinking and writing through debates: An experimental evaluation. *Teaching Sociology, 18*(4), 462–471.

Green, E. (2014, July 23). Why do Americans stink at math? *The New York Times*. Retrieved from http://www.nytimes.com/2014/07/27/magazine/why-do-americans-stink-at-math.html

Green, E. (2014). *Building a better teacher: How teaching works (and how to teach it to everyone)*. New York: W. W. Norton & Company.

Gross, D., Pietri, E., Anderson, G., Moyano-Camihort, K., and Graham, M. (2015). Increased preclass preparation underlies student outcome improvement in the flipped classroom. *CBE Life Sciences Education, 14*(4). doi: 10.1187/cbe.15-02-0040

Habanek, D. V. (2005). An examination of the integrity of the syllabus. *College Teaching, 53*, 62–64.

Hake, R. R. (1998). Interactive-engagement versus traditional methods: A six-thousand-student survey of mechanics tests data for introductory physics courses. *American Journal of Physics, 66*(64). Retrieved from http://dx.doi.org/10.1119/1.18809

Hara, B. (2010, October 19). Graphic display of student learning objectives [web log post]. *ProfHacker*. Retrieved from http://www.chronicle.com/blogs/profhacker/graphic-display-of-student-learning-objectives/27863

Harnish, R. J., and Bridges, K. R. (2011). Effect of syllabus tone: Students' perceptions of instructor and course. *Social Psychology of Education, 14*(3), 319–330.

Hart Research Associates. (2015). *Falling short? College learning and career success: Selected findings from online surveys of employers and college students conducted on behalf of the Association of American Colleges and Universities.* Washington, D.C.: Author. Retrieved from https://www.aacu.org/sites/default/files/files/LEAP/2015em ployerstudentsurvey.pdf

Hart, B., and Risley, T. (2003, Spring). The early catastrophe: The 30 million word gap by age 3. *American Educator*, 4–9. Retrieved from https://www.aft.org/sites/default/files/periodicals/TheEarlyC atastrophe.pdf

Hattie, J. (2015). The applicability of Visible Learning to higher education. *Scholarship of Teaching and Learning in Psychology*, 1(1), 79–91.

Henderson, C., and Rosenthal, A. (2006). Reading questions: Encouraging students to read the text before coming to class. *Journal of College Science Teaching*, 35(7), 46–50.

Highberg, N. P. (2010, January 11). *Rid your syllabus of the passive voice* [web log post]. Retrieved from ProfHacker: http://chronicle.com/blogs/profhacker/rid-your-syllabi-of-the-passive-voice/22903

Hill, A., Arford, T., Lubitow, A., and Smollin, L. (2012). "I'm ambivalent about it": The dilemmas of PowerPoint. *Teaching Sociology*, 40(3), 242–256.

Hinds, P. J. (1999). The curse of expertise: The effects of expertise and debiasing methods on prediction of novel performance. *Journal of Experimental Psychology: Applied*, 5(2), 205–221.

Hobson, E. H. (2003, November). *Encouraging students to read required course material.* Workshop presented at the 28th Annual Conference of the Professional and Organizational Development (POD) Network in Higher Education, Denver, CO.

Hogarth, R. M., and Reder, M. W. (Eds.). (1986). The behavioral foundations of economic theory. *The Journal of Business*, 59(4), Part 2.

Honeycutt, B. (2016, July 11). Five time-saving strategies for the flipped classroom. *Faculty Focus*. Retrieved from http://www.facultyfocus.com/articles/blended-flipped-learning/five-time-saving-strategies-flipped-classroom/

Hopkins, G. (2003a). Four corners debate. *Education World*. Retrieved from http://www.educationworld.com/a_lesson/03/lp304-04.shtml

Hopkins, G. (2003b). Role play debate. *Education World*. Retrieved from http://www.educationworld.com/a_lesson/03/lp304-02.shtml

House Committee on Education and the Workforce Democratic Staff. (2014). *The just-in-time professor: A staff report summarizing eforum responses on the working conditions of contingent faculty in higher education.* Washington DC: Author. Retrieved from http://democrats-edworkforce.house.gov/imo/media/doc/1.24.14-AdjunctEforumReport.pdf

Ishiyama, J., and Hartlaub, S. (2002). Does the wording of syllabi affect student course assessment in introductory political science classes? *PS: Political Science and Politics, 35*(3), 567–570.

Johnstone, A. H., and Percival, F. (1976). Attention breaks in lectures. *Education in Chemistry, 13*, 49–50.

Kelly, K. (2016, June 23). Teaching tips to help underprepared students learn more [web log post]. *ACUE Community.* Retrieved from https://community.acue.org/blog/teaching-tips-underprepared-students-learn/

Kennedy, R. (2007). In-class debates: Fertile ground for active learning and the cultivation of critical thinking and oral communication skills. *International Journal of Teaching and Learning in Higher Education, 19*(2), 183–190. Retrieved from http://www.isetl.org/ijtlhe/pdf/IJTLHE200.pdf

Kober, N. (2015). *Reaching students: What research says about effective instruction in undergraduate science and engineering.* Washington, D.C.: National Academies Press.

Laist, R. (2015, May 11). Getting the most out of guest experts who speak to your class. *Faculty Focus*. Retrieved from http://www.facultyfocus.com/articles/curriculum-development/getting-the-most-out-of-guest-experts-who-speak-to-your-class/

Lambert, C. (2010, March–April). Nonstop: Today's superhero undergraduates do "3,000 things at 150 percent." *Harvard Magazine*. Retrieved from http://harvardmagazine.com/2010/03/nonstop

Lambert, C. (2012, March–April). Twilight of the lecture. *Harvard Magazine*. Retrieved from http://harvardmagazine.com/2012/03/twilight-of-the-lecture

Lemov, D. (2015). *Teach like a champion 2.0: 62 techniques that put students on the path to college*. San Francisco: Jossey-Bass.

Levasseur, D. G., and Sawyer, J. K. (2006). Pedagogy meets PowerPoint: A research review of the effects of computer-generated slides in the classroom. *The Review of Communication*, *6*(1/2), 101–123

Liaw, S. S. (2004). Considerations for developing constructivist web-based learning. *International Journal of Instructional Media*, *31*(3), 309–321.

Macdonald, R. H., Manduca, C. A., Mogk, D. W., and Tewksbury, B. J. (2005). Teaching methods in undergraduate geoscience courses: Results of the 2004 On the Cutting Edge Survey of U.S. faculty. *Journal of Geoscience Education*, *53*(3), 237–252.

Mann, S., and Robinson, A. (2009). Boredom in the lecture theatre: an investigation into the contributors, moderators and outcomes of boredom amongst university students. *British Educational Research Journal, 35*(2), 243–258.

Marcus, A. (ed.) (2013). *Design, user experience, and usability: Web, mobile, and product design* (Lecture Notes in Computer Science series). New York: Springer.

Marshall, P. (1974). How much, how often? *College and Research Libraries, 35*(6), 453–456.

Mayer, R. E. (2009). *Multimedia learning* (2nd ed). Cambridge, MA: Cambridge University Press.

Mayer, R. E. (2014). Research-based principles for designing multimedia instruction. In V. A. Benassi, C. E. Overson, and C. M. Hakala (Eds.). *Applying science of learning in education: Infusing psychological science into the curriculum.* Retrieved from the Society for the Teaching of Psychology web site: http://teachpsych.org/ebooks/asle2014/index.php

McGuire, S. Y., and McGuire, S. (2015). *Teach students how to learn: Strategies you can incorporate into any course to improve student metacognition, study skills, and motivation.* Sterling, VA: Stylus.

McTighe, J., and Wiggins. G. (2013). *Essential questions: Opening doors to student understanding.* Alexandria, VA: Association for Supervision & Curriculum Development.

Member, P. L. (2003, April 11). NSF grant reviewer tells all [web log post]. *Science*. Retrieved from http://www.sciencemag.org/careers/2003/04/nsf-grant-reviewer-tells-all

Metrejean, C., Pittman, J., and Zarzeski, M. (2002). Guest speakers: Reflections on the role of accountants in the classroom. *Accounting Education, 11*(4). Retrieved from http://dx.doi.org/10.1080/0963928021000031466

Meyers and Jones. (1993). *Promoting active learning: Strategies for the college classroom*. San Francisco, CA: Jossey-Bass.

Michigan State School of Journalism. (2016). *To my professor: Student voices for great college teaching*. Canton, MI: Read the Spirit Books.

Middendorf, J., and Kalish, A. (1996). The "change-up" in lectures. *National Teaching and Learning Forum, 5*(2), 1–5.

Minaker, N. (2013, March 11). My best lesson: I get my psychology students to assess my mental health. *The Guardian*. Retrieved from http://www.theguardian.com/teacher-network/teacher-blog/2013/mar/11/teaching-psychology-mental-illness-sanity-my-best-lesson

Mintz, S. (2016, March 28). Designing next-generation universities [web log post]. *Inside Higher Ed*. Retrieved from https://www.insidehighered.com/blogs/higher-ed-beta/designing-next-generation-universities

Morehead, J. (2012, June 19). Stanford University's Carol Dweck on the growth mindset and education [web log post]. *OneDublin.org*. Retrieved from https://onedublin.org/2012/06/19/stanford-universitys-carol-dweck-on-the-growth-mindset-and-education/

Muller, C. (2001). The role of caring in the teacher-student relationship for at-risk students. *Sociological Inquiry, 71*(2), 241–255. doi: 10.1111/j.1475-682X.2001.tb01110.x

Murphy, M., and Destin, M. (2016, May 18). *Promoting inclusion and identity safety to support college success (College Completion Series: Part Three)*. New York: The Century Foundation. Retrieved from https://tcf.org/content/report/promoting-inclusion-identity-safety-support-college-success

Murray, C., and Malmgren, K. (2005). Implementing a teacher-student relationship program in a high-poverty urban school: Effects on social, emotional, and academic adjustment and lessons learned. *Journal of School Psychology, 43*(2), 137–152.

Nathan, R. (2005). *My freshman year: What a professor learned by becoming a student*. Ithaca, NY: Cornell University Press.

National Research Council (1999). *How people learn: Brain, mind, experience, and school*. Washington, D.C.: National Academies Press.

Nault, K. (2014, February 17). Busy students work against time to complete daily tasks. *Daily Titan*. Retrieved from http://www.dailytitan.com/2014/02/busy-students-work-against-time-to-complete-daily-tasks/

Newbold, C. (2016, August, 16). How to write a syllabus students may actually read: Six quick tips [web log post]. *The Visual Communication Guy*. Retrieved from http://thevisualcommunicationguy.com/2016/08/16/how-to-write-a-syllabus-students-may-actually-read-six-quick-tips/

Nickerson, R. (1999). How we know—and sometimes misjudge—what others know: Imputing one's own knowledge to others. *Psychological Bulletin, 125*(6), 737–759.

Nickerson, S. (2007–2008). Role-play: An often misused active learning strategy. *Essays on Teaching Excellence* [A publication of *The Professional & Organizational Development Network in Higher Education*], *19*(5). Retrieved from http://podnetwork.org/content/uploads/V19-N5-Nickerson.pdf

Nilson, L. B. (2007). *The graphic syllabus and the outcomes map: Communicating your course.* San Francisco, CA: Jossey-Bass.

Nilson, L.B. (2010). *Teaching at its best* (3rd ed.). San Francisco, CA: Jossey-Bass.

Nisbett, R. (2009). *Intelligence and how to get it: Why schools and cultures count.* New York: W. W. Norton & Company.

Nisbett, R., and Ross, L. (1980). *Human inference: Strategies and shortcomings of social judgment.* Englewood Cliffs, NJ:

Prentice-Hall.

Oakley, B., Felder, R. M., Brent, R., and Elhajj, I. (2004). Turning student groups into effective teams. *Journal of Student Centered Learning, 2*(1), 9–34.

Pennebaker, J. W., Gosling, S. D., and Ferrell, J. D. (2013, November 20). Daily online testing in large classes: Boosting college performance while reducing achievement gaps. *PLOS.* Retrieved from ttp://dx.doi.org/10.1371/journal.pone.0079774

Pink, D. (2012). *To sell is human: The surprising truth about moving others*. New York: Riverhead Books.

Pinker, S. (2014). *The sense of style: The thinking person's guide to writing in the 21st century*. New York: Penguin Books.

Porter, R. (2005). What do grant reviewers really want, anyway? *The Journal of Research Administration, 36*(2), 5–13.

Preszler, R.W. (2009). Replacing lecture with peer-led workshops improve student learning. *CBE Life Sciences Education, 8*(3), 182–192. Retrieved from http://doi.org/10.1187/cbe.09-01-0002

PRI Public Radio International. (2009, August 18). *Ira Glass on storytelling, part 1 of 4* [Video file]. Retrieved from https://www.youtube.com/watch?v=loxJ3FtCJJA

Rodriguez, J. I., Plax, T. G., and Kearney, P. (1996). Clarifying the relationship between teacher nonverbal immediacy and student cognitive learning: Affective learning as the central causal mediator. *Communication Education, 45,* 293–305.

Roth, W.M., McRobbie, C.J., Lucas, K.B., and Boutonne. S. (1997). Why may students fail to learn from demonstrations? A social practice perspective on learning in physics. *Journal of Research in Science Teaching, 34*(5), 509–33.

Rubin, S. (1985, August 7). Professors, students, and the syllabus. *Chronicle of Higher Education.* Retrieved from http://www.colorado.edu/gtp/2013/01/29/professors-students-and-syllabus

Sanchez, C. (2015, May 8). What the best college teachers do [Conversation with Ken Bain]. *nprED.* Retrieved from http://www.npr.org/sections/ed/2015/05/08/404960905/what-the-best-college-teachers-do

Saul, W., Kohnen, A., Newman, A., and Pearce, L. (2012). *Front-page science: Engaging teens in science literacy.* Arlington, VA: NSTA Press.

Schuman, R. (2015, October 21). Professors shouldn't teach to younger versions of themselves. *Slate.* Retrieved from http://www.slate.com/articles/life/education/2015/10/professors_shouldn_t_only_teach_to_younger_versions_of_themselves.html

Schwartz, D. L., and Bransford, J. D. (1998). A time for telling. *Cognition and Instruction, 16*(4), 475–522.

Schwartz, K. (2015, September 21). 10 tips for launching an inquiry-based classroom [web log post]. *MindShift*. Retrieved from https://ww2.kqed.org/mindshift/2015/09/21/10-tips-for-launching-an-inquiry-based-classroom/

Schuman, R. (2014, March 14). PowerPointless: Digital slideshows are the scourge of higher education. *Slate*. Retrieved from http://www.slate.com/articles/life/education/2014/03/power point_in_higher_education_is_ruining_teaching.html

Selingo, J. J. (2015, January 26). Why are so many college students failing to gain job skills before graduation? *The Washington Post*. Retrieved from https://www.washingtonpost.com/news/grade-point/wp/2015/01/26/why-are-so-many-college-students-failing-to-gain-job-skills-before-graduation/

Seymour, E., and Hewitt, N. M. (1997). *Talking about leaving: Why undergraduates leave the sciences*. Boulder, CO: Westview.

Shernoff, D. (2013). *Toward an optimal learning environment: Studies of engagement at the moment of instruction*. New York: Springer.

Singer, S. R., Nielsen, N. R. and Schweingruber, H. A. (Eds). (2012). *Discipline-based education research: Understanding and improving learning in undergraduate science and engineering*. Washington, D.C.: National Academies Press.

Smith, D. J. and Valentine, T. (2012). The use and perceived effectiveness of instructional practices in two-year technical colleges. *Journal on Excellence in College Teaching, 23*(1), 133–161.

Smith, R. (2015, June 17). College doesn't prepare students for full-time jobs—internships do [commentary]. *Fortune*. Retrieved from http://fortune.com/2015/06/16/ryan-smith-internship-advice/

Stanovich, K. E. (2012). *How to think straight about psychology* (10th ed.). New York: Pearson.

Stice, J.E. (1987). Using Kolb's learning cycle to improve student learning. *Engineering Education, 77*: 291–296.

Strong, M. (1997). *The habit of thought: From Socratic seminars to Socratic practice*. Chapel Hill, NC: New View Publications.

Syverson, K. M. (2013). Sonar demonstration—Human sound wave. *On the Cutting Edge: Strong Undergraduate Geoscience Teaching*. Retrieved from http://serc.carleton.edu/NAGTWorkshops/oceanography/activities/72682.html

Tanner, K. D. (2013). Structure matters: 21 teaching strategies to promote student engagement and cultivate classroom equity. *CBE Life Sciences Education, 12*, 322-331. Retrieved from http://ctl.yale.edu/sites/default/files/basic-page-supplementary-materials-files/tanner2013cbe_2013_equitystrategies.pdf

The College Board. (n.d.). *Quick guide: Types of college courses.* Retrieved from https://bigfuture.collegeboard.org/find-colleges/academic-life/quick-guide-types-of-college-courses

The RSA. (2015, December 15). *RSA animate: How to help every child fulfill their potential* [Video file]. Retrieved from https://www.youtube.com/watch?v=Yl9TVbAal5s&feature=youtu.be

The Sheridan Center for Teaching and Learning (n.d.). *Interactive classroom activities.* Retrieved from https://www.brown.edu/about/administration/sheridan-center/teaching-learning/effective-classroom-practices/interactive-classroom-activities

Tobias, S. (1990). They're not dumb. They're different. A new tier of talent for science. *Change, 22,* 11–30.

van Hoek, R., Godsell, J., and Harrison, A. (2011). Embedding insights from industry in supply chain programmes: The role of guest lecturers. *Supply Chain Management: An International Journal, 16*(2), 142–147.

von Glasersfeld, E. (1995). A constructivist approach to teaching. In L. P. Steffe & J. Gale (Eds.), *Constructivism in education* (pp. 3–15). Hillsdale: Erlbaum.

Waldrop, M. M. (2015, July 15). Why we are teaching science wrong, and how to make it right. *Nature, 523,* 272-274. doi:10.1038/523272a. Retrieved from http://www.nature.com/news/why-we-are-teaching-science-wrong-and-how-to-make-it-right-1.17963#/ref-link-1

Warner, J. (2016, January 18). When students won't do the reading [web log post]. *Inside Higher Ed.* Retrieved from https://www.insidehighered.com/blogs/just-visiting/when-students-wont-do-reading

Weimer, M. (2002). *Learner-centered teaching: Five key changes to practice.* San Francisco: Jossey-Bass.

Weimer, M. (2012, May 2). A graphic syllabus can bring clarity to course structure [web log post]. *Faculty Focus.* Retrieved from http://www.facultyfocus.com/articles/teaching-professor-blog/a-graphic-syllabus-can-bring-clarity-to-course-structure/

Weissman, J. (2008). *Presenting to win: The art of telling your story.* Upper Saddle River, NJ: FT Press.

Westervelt, E. (2016, April 14). A Nobel laureate's higher education plea: Revolutionize teaching. *NPR.* Retrieved from http://www.npr.org/sections/ed/2016/04/14/465729968/a-nobel-laureates-education-plea-revolutionize-teaching

Whitney, H. M (2010, June 24). *Choosing the right 'person' in classroom communication* [web log post]. Retrieved from ProfHacker: http://chronicle.com/blogs/profhacker/choosing-the-right-person-in-classroom-communication/24931

Wieman, C. E. (2014). Large-scale comparison of science teaching methods sends clear message [Commentary]. *Proceedings of the National Academy of Sciences of the United States of America*, 111(23), 8319-8320. Retrieved from http://www.pnas.org/content/111/23/8319.full.pdf

Wiggins, G., and McTighe, J. (1998). *Understanding by design*. Alexandria, VA: Association for Supervision and Curriculum Development.

Yager, R. (2015). The role of exploration in the classroom (STEM). In A. Ornstein and N. Eng (Eds.), "21st Century Excellence in Education," *Society, 52*, 210–218.

Yale Center for Teaching and Learning. (n.d.). *Public speaking for teachers II: The mechanics of speaking*. Retrieved from http://ctl.yale.edu/teaching/ideas-teaching/public-speaking-teachers-ii-mechanics-speaking

Zamudio-Suaréz, F. (2016, August 31). Is anybody reading the syllabus? To find out, some professors bury hidden gems. *The Chronicle of Higher Education*. Retrieved from http://www.chronicle.com/article/Is-Anybody-Reading-the/237641

Zorek, J. A., Katz, N. L., and Popovich, N. G. (2011). Guest speakers in a professional development seminar series. *American Journal of Pharmaceutical Education, 75*(2), Article 28.

ABOUT THE AUTHOR

Norman Eng is a doctor of education (Ed.D.) with a background in teaching and marketing—two areas that relate to lecturing, presenting, and engaging audiences.

As a marketing executive, he worked with clients to realize their communication goals in the pharmaceutical, insurance, pet, and retail industries. Norman learned one major lesson, something he discusses in Chapter 2: *Know your target audience.*

He applied this lesson to his teaching as a public school elementary school teacher in the early- to mid-2000s, where he was nominated as one of Honor Roll's Outstanding American Teachers.

As an adjunct assistant professor for local colleges in the City University of New York system, Norman realized that much of what he gained as a marketer *and* as an elementary school teacher held true for college instructors: Students—whether undergraduate or graduate—need to see the value of what you are teaching to their lives. With consistently high student and departmental evaluations in two separate colleges every semester, Dr. Eng hopes to share what he has gained so far from these three industries—marketing, K–12 education, and higher education—with the larger community of higher education instructors, whether they are graduate students, adjunct lecturers, assistant professors, or beyond.

ENDNOTES

1. See for example Lambert (2010) and Nault (2014)

2. Eagan et al. (2014)

3. See, for example, Bligh (1971); Freeman, Eddy, McDonough, Smith, Okoroafor, Jordt, and Wenderoth (2014); Smith and Valentine (2012)

4. See American Association of University Professors (n.d.). According to PBS, the rate is 70 percent (see Fruscione, 2014)

5. House Committee on Education and the Workforce Democratic Staff (2014)

6. CareerBuilder (2015); see also Friedman (2013), Selingo (2015), and Smith (2015)

7. Hart Research Associates (2015)

8. Andrews, Leonard, Colgrove, and Kalinowsky (2011)

9. Lambert, 2012

10. IBID, para. 18 (Lambert)

11. Bligh (1971)

12. Stice (1987)

13. Meyers and Jones (1993)

14. Schuman (2015)

[15] Burns (1985); Gage (1976); Goodman (2006); Johnstone and Percival (1976); Middendorf and Kalish (1996)

[16] Meyers and Jones (1993)

[17] Pinker (2014)

[18] Hinds (1999); Hogarth (1986); Nickerson (1999)

[19] Committee on Developments in the Science of Learning et al. (2000)

[20] Hill, Arford, Lubitow, and Smollin (2012)

[21] Hill et al. (2012), pp. 251–252

[22] Carolyn Works (2009)

[23] Mann and Robinson (2009)

[24] Foote (2010), p. 460

[25] Pink (2012), p. 136

[26] Barone et al. (2016) para. 16

[27] Retelling of Leo Lionni's *Fish is Fish* by Bransford, Brown, and Cocking (2000)

[28] Ambrose et al. (2010)

[29] Bain (2004)

[30] Wiggins and McTighe (1998)

[31] Kelly (2016); Nilson (2010)

[32] Bain (2004); Sanchez (2015)

[33] Freeman et al. (2014); Hake (1998); Eddy and Hogan (2014); Kober (2015)

[34] Mintz (2016)

[35] Lambert (2012) para. 27

[36] Westervelt (2016)

[37] Ibid, para. 10

[38] Lambert (2012), para. 14

[39] Fosnot (1996); von Glasersfeld (1995)

[40] Green (2014)

[41] Bain (2004)

[42] Waldrop (2015). (Ibid)

[43] Westervelt (2016)

[44] Duch, Groh, and Allen (2001)

[45] Yager (2015); Saul et al. (2012)

[46] Schwartz and Bransford (1998)

[47] Boaler (2016), p. 68

[48] Minaker (2013)

[49] Bain (2004), p. 28

[50] See Johnson (2006):
http://www.ncbi.nlm.nih.gov/pmc/articles/PMC2384173/

[51] Porter (2005), p. 7

[52] Member (2003).

[53] Ibid, p. 8

[54] Ibid, p. 9

[55] Newbold (2016)

[56] Wiggins and McTighe (1998)

[57] Rubin (1985)

[58] Bart (2015)

[59] Marcus (2013); Newbold (2016)

[60] Newbold (2016)

[61] Allan, Clarke, and Jopling (2009); Harnish and Bridges (2011); Ishiyama and Hartlaub (2002)

[62] Some ideas were adapted from
https://accessiblesyllabus.tulane.edu/

[63] See Highberg (2010) and Whitney (2010)

[64] See http://www.syllabusinstitute.org/wp-content/uploads/2011/10/Cost-of-Syllabi-White-Paper.pdf

[65] For an example, see Hara (2010):
http://www.chronicle.com/blogs/profhacker/graphic-display-of-

student-learning-objectives/27863; for more information on how a graphic syllabus can improve your syllabi, see Nilson (2007) and Weimer (2012). Be careful to make graphics easy to understand.

66 For a concise breakdown of a jigsaw activity, see: https://www.cte.cornell.edu/teaching-ideas/designing-your-course/writing-a-syllabus.html

67 Zamudio-Suaréz (2016)

68 Mayer (2009)

69 Seymour and Hewitt (1997); Tobias (1990)

70 Bain (2004); Goodman (2006)
71 National Research Council (1999); AAAS (2011)

72 Finley (2016)

73 McTighe and Wiggins (2013)

74 Ambrose et al. (2010); National Research Council (1999)

75 Gawande (2013)

76 Budesheim and Lundquist (2000); Green and Klug (1990)

77 Kennedy (2007)

78 See http://archive.wceruw.org/cl1/cl/moreinfo/MI3D.htm

79 Bargh and Schul (1980)

80 Aronson and Patnoe (2011); see also https://www.jigsaw.org/

81 Oakley, Felder, Brent, and Elhajj (2004)

[82] Lemov (2015)

[83] See http://surfaquarium.com/MI/inventory.htm

[84] See https://sites.sas.upenn.edu/duckworth/pages/research

[85] Nickerson (2007-08)

[86] Ibid

[87] Hopkins (2003b)

[88] Syverson (2013)

[89] Allain (2011); see https://www.wired.com/2011/10/how-to-model-newtons-cradle/

[90] Crouch et al. (2004); Roth et al. (1997)

[91] See http://www.stanford.edu/dept/CTL/cgi-bin/docs/newsletter/case_studies.pdf

[92] Foran (2001)

[93] Metrejean, Pittman, and Zarzeski (2002); van Hoek et al. (2011); Zorek, Katz, and Popovich (2011)

[94] Laist (2015)

[95] Gage (1976)

[96] Atkinson (2005); Weissman (2008)

[97] Weissman (2008); Yale Center for Teaching and Learning (n.d.)

[98] Adapted from Weissman (2008)

[99] Mayer (2009)

[100] Mayer (2014)

[101] Ibid

[102] See https://creativecommons.org/about/program-areas/education-oer/education-oer-resources/

[103] Schwartz (2015)

[104] PRI Public Radio International (2009)

[105] Hart and Risley (2003)

[106] Cron (2012); Fryer (2003)

[107] Bakhtin (1981), pp. 293–294

[108] Fisher, Frey, and Rothenberg (2008)

[109] Flanders (1970)

[110] Anderson and Krathwohl (2001)

[111] Strong (1997), p. 55

[112] Nisbett and Ross (1980); Stanovich (2012)

[113] Rubin (1985)

[114] Duhigg (2016)

[115] Allan, Clarke, and Jopling (2009), pp. 366, 368

[116] Based on the work of DeSurra and Church (1994)

[117] DeSurra and Church (1994)

[118] Seymour and Hewitt (1997)

[119] Gehlbach and Robinson (2016); Muller (2001); Murray and Malmgren (2005)

[120] Chambliss (2014); Michigan State School of Journalism (2016)

[121] Tanner (2013)

[122] Gonzalez (2015)

[123] Dweck (2006)

[124] The RSA (2015)

[125] Nisbett (2009)

[126] The RSA (2015)

[127] Morehead (2012)

[128] Chesler, Wilson, and Malani (1993)

[129] Warner (2016)

[130] e.g., Burchfield & Sappington (2000); Hobson (2003); Marshall (1974)

[131] Cathy Small published under a pseudonym, Rebekah Nathan (2005), to protect her subjects' identities.

[132] Based on the motivation research by Ambrose et al. (2010)

[133] Henderson and Rosenthal (2006)

[134] Ibid; Warner (2016)

[135] Angelo and Cross (1993)

[136] The Sheridan Center for Teaching and Learning (n.d.)

[137] Bransford, Brown, and Cocking (2000)

[138] Ambrose et al. (2010), pp. 150–151

[139] Hattie (2015)

[140] Allan, Clarke, and Jopling (2009); Bloxham and West (2007)

[141] McGuire and McGuire (2015)

[142] Oakley et al. (2004)

[143] Lemov (2015)

[144] Dallimore, Hertenstein, and Platt (2013)

[145] Ibid

[146] Downey (2016)

[147] Delpit (1995)

[148] Adapted from Eng (2016)

YOUR VOICE IS IMPORTANT.

I appreciate hearing from you.

What was useful? What can make this book even better?
Your feedback is invaluable for the next edition of this book.

Please leave me a helpful review on Amazon letting me know.

Thanks so much.

Norman Eng

75342333R00192

Made in the USA
Columbia, SC
16 August 2017